Riches to Rags

Copyright © 1984

Schenkman Publishing Company, Inc.
Box 1570
Cambridge, MA 02138

Library of Congress Cataloging in Publication Data

Dovring, Folke.
  Riches to rags.

  1. Waste (Economics)—United States. 2. United
States—Economic conditions—1981– . 3. United
States—Social conditions—1980– . I. Title.
II. Title: Social waste.
HC110.W3D68   1984   330.973'0927   84-5406
ISBN 0-87073-514-4
ISBN 0-87073-515-2 (pbk.)
Printed in the United States of America

All rights reserved. This book, or parts thereof,
may not be reproduced in any form without written
permission from the publisher.

Riches to Rags:
The Political Economy of Social Waste

by

Folke Dovring

SCHENKMAN PUBLISHING COMPANY, INC.
Cambridge, Massachusetts

ROBERT MANNING
LIBRARY

JAN 13 1986

Tallahassee, Florida

Soc
HC
110
W3
D68
1984

Table of Contents

Preface: Waste and the National Destiny	ix
Chapter 1. Economics of Redundancy	1
Scarcity and wealth	1
Social waste in America	3
Waste and employment	4
Luxury and excess capacity	6
National income	7
Energy and manpower: The lock-in systems	8
Chapter 2. Our Daily Bread and How It Is Buttered	11
Bread and pigs' feed	12
The fat of the land	16
The meat of the problem	19
Chapter 3. Money to Burn: Oil Waste in America	25
Fuel Waste in the United States and in other countries	25
Consumption versus capital formation	27
Oil crisis, inflation, and recession	29
Oil and investment	32
Time trends in the United States	33
Effects on the world of United States consumption habits	35
OPEC and United States oil interests	35
Choices of the 1950's and the 1980's	36
Roots of improvidence	39
A partisan issue?	41
Chapter 4. Curse in Disguise: The Car in America	43
Freedom from horses	43
Freedom of cars	45
Free from timetables, shackled to the wheel	47
Loss of options, loss of efficiency	49

Hazardous to your life and health	52
Finding a way out of the maze	53

Chapter 5. From Community to Traffic Machine:
Disintegration of the American City	55
America the rural	56
Old cities and new	56
H.U.D. and the highway system	58
City layout and energy waste	61
Commuter traffic	63
Shopping traffic and car-free zones	64
Parking areas and alternative land use	65
Blighted areas, blighted people	67

Chapter 6. From Prohibition to Drug War	71
Prohibition and syndicate crime	71
Demand creates supply	72
Supply creates demand	73
Scarcity is good for business	74
Rich crooks, poor police	75
Successful Mafia, weaker society	77
A road to sanity: Education	78

Chapter 7. Schoolroom Boredom and Pap Entertainment	81
The tribal school	82
The liberal ideal	83
Schoolroom collective	86
Classroom teaching is low productive	87
The more the worse	89
Fill the time, waste the talent	90
Anthill drill versus mental unfolding	91
From conformism to vulgarity	93
A shift of emphasis	95

Chapter 8. Discrimination and the Waste of Talent	99
A matter of fair competition	99
Technical competence	100
Leadership and managerial competence	105
Variety of talent	106
Competitive justice	110

    Penalties for discrimination. 111
    Running just to stay in place?. 113

Chapter 9. Defense Sinkhole 115
    Defense as an economic sinkhole 116
    The sinkhole deepens. 118
    Cost overruns, obsolescence and redundancy 119
    Nuclear overkill. 120
    Economic stabilizer 122
    Technicological Spinoffs 124
    Stability, superiority, and small gangsters. 125
    No end in sight 127

Chapter 10. The Conditions for Unlimited Economic
               Growth. 129
    Meaning of economic growth. 130
    Value and Volume 130
    Production and environment 131
    Hidden productivity gains: Cost of production versus
        value in use 132
    Population control 134
    No limitless energy. 136
    Demand saturation. 137
    Substitution of matter for matter 138
    Substitution of design for matter 139
    Access and use 141

Chapter 11. Back to Supply-Side Waste. 143
    Back to the market 144
    Business as government 145
    Supply-side capital 147
    Rich savers, poor wasters? 150
    Energy and capital 152
    Money and goods 153
    A worsening social structure 154
    Wishful thinking, vested interests, and inertia. 156

Chapter 12. . . . Or Forward to a Sane Society? 157
    A market concept of planning 157
    Oil, cars, and cities: The economic equivalent of war . . . 158

Equality of Rights: A matter of law and money 163
Poverty: Waste and riot hazards 164
Drugs and discipline: The social equivalent of peace.... 165
Education, research, and culture: Purpose over
    paycheck... 167
Food and all that: A plea for market neutrality......... 169
In defense of defense................................ 169
By the skin of our teeth—or the power of our minds? .. 170

Preface
Waste and the National Destiny

Social waste in America is as old as the country itself. Imported talent and imported technology met with natural resources so ample that it seemed of little consequence that both talent and natural resources were wasted on a grand scale. Rapid progress got the appearance of being furthered by wasteful use of both resources and people. Or at least, it seemed as if the waste did not matter. In splendid isolation, the country could steer ahead of the world, caring not much except for its success stories.

Now however, we are facing limits in this shrinking world. A new kind of ingenuity is needed. Oil and gas will run out in America, later also in the world. The energy problem becomes one of rising costs, above all capital costs. At the same time, our modern economy needs more and more quality manpower, we can no longer afford to waste potential talent by discrimination, shoddy education, drug abuse, or deepening poverty.

But public policy does not seem to live up to these challenges. What goes by the label of Conservatism will only render the problems worse by postponing indispensable reforms. Social waste is at the root of the recession syndrome of recent years. If it is not checked, recession may become permanent and lead to continuous deterioration of the national fabric.

Nothing is inevitable unless we believe it to be so. To tackle the problems caused by social waste, we must first learn to know about that condition itself. It will not go away by wishful thinking.

Chapter 1
Economics of Redundancy

When things of value are destroyed or used up to no purpose, we know this as waste. Social waste is harder to recognize than individual waste. It often occurs while some individuals are gaining at the expense of others and of society as a whole. Individual gains and losses are easier to spot than are losses to society. Yet, if we take the trouble to look at how things work in our society, we shall discover that social waste is a large and pervasive force, a weakening influence on the nation as a whole.

Social waste is used consciously, and on a large scale, to sustain prices of things which tend to become less scarce and less expensive. Such waste hurts society as a whole and most of its members, but it favors those who own the resources that are wasted. Food, clothing, housing and transportation are all used wastefully so that owners of land, mines, oil wells, and other basic resources may get a larger share of the nation's income in exchange for what they have to sell. Talented people among women and minorities are also wasted so that those in favored positions—white males—may suffer less competition and hence get more for their talent because it is more scarce under discrimination. There is no end to the things that can be wasted whenever some favored group can arrange this in its own perceived interest.

SCARCITY AND WEALTH

Riches can be embarrassing. Unexpected abundance is often treated as a scourge worse than the scarcity we are all accustomed to. Farmers know this all too well; whenever the harvest is more bountiful than the market will take, collapsing prices threaten them with ruin. Economics is the "dismal science" of how to live with scarcity. Whenever scarcity is relaxed, economics and business tend to come together to introduce it anew. If scarcity is not there to begin with, it is invented on purpose, by creating redundancies.

Scarcity is not only the reason for Economics; it is also its main steering force. Things in abundance, such as air and sunshine, have no price and are not traded on markets. They belong to no one, and they also support no economic doctrine—as long as they remain abundant. Economic goods—those that are produced for sale and are bought for consumption or investment—are scarce by definition. Scarcity forces us to act with economic rationality and to spend our limited means on those goods and services for which we have an economic demand, and in proportion (between these goods and services) to how much we value them. Thus supply and demand are brought into equilibrium, a state of affairs around which Economics builds its doctrine.

What would happen if many scarce goods were to become abundant over night? Affluence by low prices would be defeated by chaos. For the economy—the system of exchange between persons, firms and governments—to function smoothly, it should be close to equilibrium, most of the time at least. Sudden changes are always upsetting, so changes have to be gradual. This gives the cue to resource owners as to how they can create redundancies and so avoid the consequences of declining costs and prices. Without counter moves by resource owners, many of them would cease to be rich, even as the general public would be better off. Owners of anything that is scarce must therefore wish that it continues to be scarce. They can further their interests by promoting more consumption of the goods they have to sell, or by holding out of the market some competing goods, as in the case of talent held down by discrimination. The result of such manipulation of consumer (and investor) demand is social waste.

There are many examples of declining scarcity and of the effect this has, and how such situations were faced. In an extreme instance, a technological innovation may be so superior that it sweeps away the more expensive goods it replaces, without meeting serious resistance. An example is the replacement of cochineal, a textile dyestuff, by artificial red dye. Cochineal comes from an insect living on cactuses, mainly in Mexico. For a long time this dye substance was a mainstay of Mexico's export trade. Then, in the late 1800's, some European chemist invented a synthetic substitute (fuchsine, rosaniline) which does the same service but costs but a fraction of what the natural article costs. Very soon, natural cochineal ceased to be harvested and Mexico lost one of its most valuable export items. If it had been possible to prevent the substitute from being produced and marketed—if this had been done in the interest of Mexico—then buyers of clothes would have continued to pay higher prices for fabrics requiring this kind of dye. In this case, such social waste was avoided because the difference was very large, and also because the substitute belonged to the economically stronger party to the conflict.

A different case of facing increased abundance is the current diamond market. Gem diamonds are not consumed and seldom lost, so the inventory is rising. Supply from new sources—among them the Soviet Union, soon also Australia—threatens to depress prices to the level of semi-precious stones. A price collapse has long been avoided by the arrangement of a single monopoly headquartered in London handling nearly all new supply, even that from the Soviet Union. But the continuing sales pitch about diamonds as a safe investment is less and less convincing. The market shows that privately owned diamonds are seldom sold for anywhere near what they were bought for. In this game of price manipulation, the winners are the miners and traders in diamonds who become parasites on society to the extent they oversupply an overpriced market. The losers are all those who are still led to believe in diamonds as an investment "forever". The longer the collapse of the diamond market is postponed the more serious it is likely to become.

These two cases were chosen as illustration because they are extreme. Most of the time, we have to probe harder to discover the existence and the extent of social waste.

SOCIAL WASTE IN AMERICA

Social waste has been, and is, more widespread in the United States than in the Old World. The vast resources of the North American continent encouraged, early on, waste rather than thrifty use. Farmlands in eastern states such as Pennsylvania and the Carolinas were "mined" for virgin soil fertility and then often abandoned for richer, more untouched lands farther to the west. Immigrants from Europe "filled in" where native Americans were leaving and began restoring the depleted lands. Rapid exploitation of mines and oil wells was for a long time encouraged systematically by special provisions such as the mining claims on public lands and the oil depletion allowance. This was done to accelerate development. It might have made some sense as long as extraction touched but a small fraction of the fixed mineral treasures, but not after it reached large proportions. A lavish transportation system has been put in place to make sure that abundant fuel and hardware would be used up as fast as they could be supplied and so sustain prices. The food system is also riddled with waste designed to increase consumption (or the appearance of it) and relieve the market glut of farm goods.

The educational system of this country is a prime example of social waste. It is over endowed with resources both material and human and yet it never seems to get enough funds because much of the funds are used in ways which are self defeating. The suffocating effect of too much classroom sitting is depressing on the development of both mind and character, and this can only be made worse by throwing more money at the system. The skimpy results which both primary and secondary schools achieve in many of their charges point to something being seriously wrong. Teaching of card games and checkers and other dubious educational practices may be on their way out, but many class routines continue to be low productive. The dichotomy of private versus mass education reinforces class barriers and makes easier to continue long standing discrimination against ethnic minorities. The winners of this system of social waste are the favored classes, and also special groups such as school administrators (most of them white men) and firms supplying textbooks and other school requisites.

WASTE AND EMPLOYMENT

Each time we attempt to argue against a case of social waste, we run into concerns for employment. Wasteful food habits help farmers, flour millers, meat packers, food retailers and their employees. Wasteful transportation helps automobile workers and a host of others—one-sixth of the employment in this country is tied directly or indirectly to the "automotive complex". Wasteful schools employ great numbers of teachers and help sustain employment in the graphic industries and publishing firms, to say nothing of textbook writers and janitors. And so on.

Anything we spend money on sustains some employment. So do, of course, also all public expenditures including that ultimate sinkhole for resources, the defense establishment. Ironically, if we follow the pro-employment argument far enough we shall discover that inefficiency employs more people than does efficiency. This is proverbial in public administration but it is seldom mentioned in connection with the automobile. For public administration, "Parkinson's Law" has become a byword and a jibe. In industry, resistance against higher efficiency was rife already more than a century and a half ago in England with the Luddite movement—described, among other places, in Charlotte Brontë's novel *Shirley*. The argument keeps coming up time and again.

The arguments in favor of wasteful employment relate only to the short-run advantage of the people currently employed in these lines of production—those intended for wasteful consumption. The logic of these arguments is false, however. Whenever we try to imagine some kind of waste cut down, we not only would reduce some current employment. We would also set free some resources which can be used to increase our total satisfactions, and to increase the employment in producing those other satisfactions. Eating less wastefully would save land for a healthier landscape and for benign energy sources. We would also save fuel and chemicals for other uses and for a less polluted environment, and we would save labor for work on something else. Using transportation less wastefully would free hardware, fuel and manpower to do things we now "can not afford" such as better equipment in health care. Even the military complex could easier have its bill of goods and personnel filled with less economic strain if there were less waste in the civilian economy, to say nothing of the military itself or of the cost overruns in the defense industries. With less wasteful mass education there could be more resources for individual self education by those who really can use it, regardless of sex or other grounds for discrimination.

The argument that waste stimulates the economy has been made many times, mostly to excess. A dramatic case is Jett Rink, the upstart Texas oil millionaire in Edna Ferber's novel *Giant*. He spent much of his new-found wealth wastefully and so put some people to work, directly and indirectly. This is in fact no different from the now classical Keynesian advice for stimulating an underemployed economy. In the extreme case, Keynes found it useful that the unemployed dig holes in the ground and fill them up again; then they would at least have something to eat. It is a valid policy when factors of production—especially labor—are under utilized but not in times of full employment. But we do not have to waste resources in order to stimulate the economy. It can also be done by printing more money. In fact, the Texas oil windfall *was* more money; the fact that this new money had a physical counterpart in more oil is economically relevant only to the extent that the new-found oil was used with economic rationality, to increase real production intended for real purposes. To the extent the new oil was wasted—as a stimulus—it was no more beneficial than new paper money.

How is it possible that the economy of the country can be riddled with social waste, and so little of this comes to the attention of the general public? In part this is because we have been trained to think in ways which accept the waste for the sake of progress it is purported to bring along. Comparisons with other advanced countries show that a high level of living does not require as much waste as we have.

Our thinking habits on social waste depend in part on the difficulty of understanding what goes on. For one thing, not all luxury is waste. An argument can also be made for some degree of excess capacity, as insurance against unexpected events. It is also difficult always to understand what national income is—social waste is a matter of how social product is used. We should realize also that wasteful habits often become institutionalized as part of a "multiple lock-in" system where the parts keep each other gripped in ways that make the system hard to break—so much so that it gets the appearance of being both rational and generally desired. Passive habits shade over into active demand.

LUXURY AND EXCESS CAPACITY

Many people like to indulge in quantitative luxuries which they could do without if they had to, or if they had more refined tastes. Big steaks, plenty of motoring for motoring's sake, large houses and other such luxuries are regarded as legitimate private demand. As long as people have such a demand for such consumption, without undue constraint or pressure, we assume that it is the economy's task to supply these goods. That is, to the extent of effective demand as defined by individuals' purchasing power and demand preferences. Luxuries are not in themselves waste; to some extent it is necessary that we should have some luxuries as escape valves from routine and collective constraints, and from life's pressures generally. But luxuries become waste when the economic and commercial system turn putative luxuries into virtual necessities which have to be consumed—for lack of viable alternatives above all, but also because of social pressures and other motives which do not really satisfy the unconstrained consumer. Here we have a large gray area in which many current economic demands might be changed if the economic policy of the country were otherwise than it is, and if new policy signals (in taxation, subsidies, etc.) were conceived intelligently enough to have real leverage. For instance, the automobile transportation system in America includes a great deal of enforced social waste. There is much of it also in other lines of consumption, as we shall see in the following. Force of habit can turn into a semblance of positive acceptance as with the long-term prison inmate who finds himself no longer able to live "on the outside".

The argument is often made that living with redundancies can have a rational purpose: because excessive capacity can come in handy in critical situations. A tightly fitted scarcity household is more vulnerable to incidental shocks than one with resources to spare. For instance, America at the eve of World War II was better equipped than other nations to throw its industry into war production because there was so much industry which could be turned around. The argument may have made some sense at the time— but for the last time. From now on we must acknowledge two other things about excess capacity. One is that the rational need for it can be calculated and in fact usually is, both in industry and insurance. For instance, the need for carry-over stocks of wheat, corn, soybeans etc. is known—we know what the likely swings are in annual harvests and how much of the crop therefore need to be kept in storage. To keep much more would be costly and would therefore defeat the purpose. The other thing is that in reality, we can better afford the carryover stocks and other excess capacity that we rationally need if we have less social waste. Continuing waste makes it more difficult to hold the margins of safety that we should have.

NATIONAL INCOME

There are some subtle problems here, of which more will be said in Chapter 10. We are told, and very often, how much the national income (or some related concept, such as Gross Domestic Product) amounts to, but the public is seldom given any explanation of what national income is or what it means.

National accounts measure products by the cost of supplying them, not by their usefulness. The matter is further complicated by intricate problems of measurement. But here we must insist on the definition: cost, not use. Goods that become cheaper tend to weigh less heavily in national accounts than those that remain expensive. A pound of butter weighs heavier in national income than a pound of high-quality margarine, and so on. Gas guzzling cars are also more impressive in conventional accounting than small, energy efficient ones: one person-mile in a gas guzzler costs more, hence represents a larger amount of national income. "Mini-cars make mini-profits" is a jibe attributed to Mr. Henry Ford, II. Whoever said it would have trouble explaining the profits made by German, Japanese and Swedish car makers. The examples can be multiplied at will. The central point is that continuing social waste is reflected in a semblance of high national income which the nation should not be interested in. Real benefits to consumers, and to the country as a whole, may therefore change in ways which are not entirely the same as the changes in national income as conventionally defined and measured.

ENERGY AND MANPOWER: THE LOCK-IN SYSTEMS

Waste in America has been debated many times but usually, as in Vance Packard's *The Waste Makers* (1960), mainly from the consumer end: ultimately, says Packard, most Americans become waste makers. References to the systematic promotion of waste, on the part of producers and resource owners, are in general either vague or anecdotal. Our main theme in this book is to show how waste is enforced by built-in constraints which often leave the individual little or no choice. To the extent the choice is really the consumer's to make freely, many types of waste have been eliminated or reduced. Packard's book, and the consumer movement, may well have contributed to a gradually more enlightened attitude toward avoidable waste—the kinds that it is in the individual's power to avoid.

The built-in waste-enforcing mechanisms are another matter. They form coherent webs, "multiple lock-in systems" which are not easily broken by individuals or individual firms, or even by communities acting in isolation from other communities. Such mechanisms are politically motivated and are reinforced because society can not afford multiple systems functioning side by side. A system in place often prevents alternatives from coming up, just because it is in place.

Enforced social waste in America is now a much more serious problem than before because of the twin problems of energy and quality manpower. The resource crisis in energy production leads to higher costs of energy, above all higher capital costs and greater logistic problems in the building up of new energy systems even as the old ones continue to occupy much of the market and to hold much of the market power. Conventional economic analysis appears at a loss to explain how we may extricate ourselves from the depressing economic effects of the energy problem when it is left without adequate attention. At the same time the lingering habits of discrimination and of routine job classifications make it more difficult to tap the entire pool of potential talent in the nation. Here also, as in energy, entrenched interests combine with inertia and the difficulty to re-design the entire social system in forcing us to waste much of the resources we have.

It is no exaggeration to say that much of the waste in America is a matter of political economy. Typically, favored groups in society tend to defend their favored positions even when this is not in the nation's interest; in doing so they also tend to have a greater material means at their disposal than do those who seek to reform the system. Solutions to such problems can not be expected from routine market forces but will have to be found on the political level. Acting as citizens and voters we can change things which are out of our reach as individual consumers.

The following chapters will treat a selection of cases where social waste is important; the catalog can not be made complete. Chapter 2 deals with waste in the food system, mainly because some examples of this are particularly easy to discuss. Chapters 3, 4 and 5 concentrate on the energy problem and its ramifications into traffic and urban problems. Chapters 6, 7 and 8 are meant to highlight several cases of waste which reduce the human potential of the nation. The specific problem of defense expenditures is treated in Chapter 9, followed by three chapters which endeavor to explain systematically what is done and what might be done about the problems debated in this book.

Chapter 2
Our Daily Bread and How It Is Buttered

American agriculture is highly efficient. No other continent (except Australia-New Zealand) can rival the efficiency of North American farmers. They are efficient at producing the goods they produce. How efficient this is to society depends on how the goods are used.

The food system includes a good deal of social waste. It is by far not the worst case of social waste in this country. It is dwarfed by the oil-and-car complex and by the denial of equal rights, probably also by both education and the drug repression system. Treating the food waste in some detail here is not intended to single it out for special attention. Rather, some of the cases of social waste in the food system are easier to visualize than some other cases to be discussed in this book.

If North Americans were eating corn, as Latin Americans do, the people of the United States could be fed from the land of Iowa, or of Illinois, or a combination of Indiana and Nebraska, for instance. That is of course far from what happens. All the immense food bounty of this vast and richly-endowed land does "clear the market" in one way or another, if sometimes with a little assistance from the Federal government and its programs to curb surplus production. A minor portion is exported, and a still lesser part of the nation's food is imported. Most of the harvest finds its way into food and fiber for 230 million Americans, where thrifty Asians could feed a billion mouths (or more) from the same amount of land, water, fertilizers, and other resources for production.

This is not to argue that the best food standard is the most austere one that would let us live and stay healthy. We will respect the economic demand for luxury, as long as it is genuine and enlightened demand. Our high-protein, high-cholesterol diets are of course by no means the most healthy regimen that could be devised for us. But that is not even the core of the problem of social waste of agricultural products. The paradox of abundance going to waste is in the "supply-side" economics of American agriculture; because the goods are produced, ways must be found to have them consumed. The self-interest of farmers led, among other things, to one of the more heartening cases of re-distributive economic policy: the American food stamp program which a reactionary government dare not attack in principle, only in extent. But this is a quantitative variation on a food system which is wasteful in many ways, even in the goods it delivers by way of food stamps. The prevalence of supply over demand was sharply highlighted in the recent program of giving away government owned cheese to needy people. This cheese is given away because it is there and because it embarrasses the government by high costs of storage; the need of the poor is not the main reason.

BREAD AND PIGS' FEED

The notion that abundant food must be used wastefully is not an exclusive for North America. Eruope has had even more shocking examples. French farm interests, more than a hundred years ago, began pressing for white bread as a prestige food because it would consume more wheat which was increasingly in excess on large French farms. Feeding the bran to pigs would fetch more money for the wheat because more of it would be used up to make white bread. Those who could not afford white bread were no help to the wheat farmers. Only a less unequal distribution of income could have made all the wheat clear the market as dark bread. This was in the same phase of Europe's economic history when English working people were given bread baked from a mixture of flour and "bakers' stuff", a mineral powder without any food value which cost less than flour and would help fill a belly without nourishing the body. Working people could not afford the real thing; those who could were seduced, by advertisements appealing to snobbery and soft tastes, into eating a product which left the best part to the pigs. The bran has most of the vitamins and mineral nutrients, and a good deal of the protein, in wheat. Thus markets were cleared without violating the social commands of an established order which found it useful that common people should be forced to work by the pressure of hunger.

In America it was never quite as crude as that. Our social waste in food stems more directly from embarassing abundance and the wish to make farm products clear the markets. Maintaining social discipline by maintaining want was not an intentional part of the system.

American bread may seem like a different story than in France, but only on the surface. Supermarkets abound in dark bread—whole wheat, cracked wheat, pumpernickel and many other special bakes are available almost everywhere. But if you read the lists of ingredients, the first one mentioned is always white flour. So the dark bread is seldom all dark. How dark is it? And how much is there of it?

Some of the answers are found in the Census of Manufactures. Under "Bakeries", we find a long list of products classified as "Bread, cake, and related products", and as "cookies and crackers". Some things are not sufficiently specified to show their contents but among those that are, we find "whole wheat, cracked wheat, and other dark breads". In terms of weight, the dark breads represented 6.8 percent of all wheat and rye breads in 1972 and 11.6 percent in 1977. A small fraction—smaller than many would expect—but rising in recent years indicating that current consumer demand may not be entirely in harmony with industrial tradition. There was some decline in rye bread. Some categories containing dark flour also went down, thus "brown and serve rolls". Among "crackers and pretzels", an item called "Graham crackers" also was smaller in 1977 than in 1972. No matter how the figures are turned around, one wonders why it took so long to respond to an obvious consumer demand.

But then we turn to look at the flour mills, in the same censuses. They were grinding out 14.12 million tons (short tons, of 2000 pounds or 907 kilograms) of wheat flour (of which 12.70 million tons was for bread) in 1977, together with 4.95 million tons of wheat mill feed (meaning bran). In 1972, the same figures were 12.58 million tons of wheat flour (of which 11.48 million was for bread) and 4.25 million tons of bran. These totals include only a very small fraction of whole wheat flour: 0.14 million tons (1.1

percent of the flour) in 1977 and 0.08 million tons (0.7 percent) in 1972. The totals also include some minor amounts of other products not intended for bread, such as durum flour (for pasta—maccaroni, etc.).

Evidently, the dark bread on the grocery shelves is not very dark. Both in 1977 and 1972, dark flour represented only about one-tenth as large a part of the flour as dark bread is of the bread. The dark breads are, on the whole, only about one-tenth dark. Some more, some even less. It reminds us of the well advertised "Roman meal bread" where the advertiser takes pain to tell the public what goes into the "Roman meal" flour, but not how much of the product so described goes into the bread which borrows its name. As usual, the specification of ingredients on the package starts with "white flour".

In most of the wheat milling, the bran is separated to be used as livestock feed. The Census of Manufactures also shows the industries which process livestock feed as purchasing nearly all the bran which the flour mills produce. The bran is about one-fourth of the weight of the wheat but contains a larger share of the mineral foods and vitamins in wheat. The price of bran, per ton, is much lower than that of white flour: not much more than half in 1977, and it was an even lesser fraction (about one-third) in 1972. Then, would not whole-wheat flour be cheaper than white flour? It contains the lower-priced component (the bran), and the milling must also be simpler and cheaper when flour and bran are not separated. Cheaper? By no means. In 1972, whole-wheat flour cost a little less than the average of all wheat flour, but not in the proportion that would follow from the prices of bran and white flour. And in 1977, whole-wheat flour was priced *higher* than white flour.

Bread prices are accordingly. In the Census, dark bread is priced 13 percent higher than white bread in 1977, 16 percent in 1972. Similar proportions (and sometimes even larger differences) can easily be verified from grocery shelves. When such perverse prices are maintained in the face of rising consumer demand for dark bread (such as it is), we can only conclude that the industries concerned (flour millers, bakers, and retailers) are biased against the product which in real terms is cheaper. They are also exploiting the rising consumer taste for it by treating dark bread as a "specialty". It is evident that they thereby are retarding the switch toward more dark bread, a switch which is desirable both for health reasons and for better resource economy.

Self interest in white bread extends to the grain farmers. More dark bread could save land and production expenditures, which is contrary to the interests of farmers and farmland owners. Bran as stockfeed could be replaced (assuming, for the moment, that the same amount of stockfeed is really needed) from feed grains, foremost corn and sorghum. The yield per area unit of these grains is generally much higher than that of wheat on the same land or on land of the same quality. In the areas where most of the bread wheat is grown, feed grains yield about twice the weight of wheat, per unit of cropland harvested. In the United States, wheat is grown on about 70 million acres each year. Saving one-fourth of it would be about 17–18 million acres, and the bran feed could be replaced from corn and sorghum grown on about half as much land, or in the vicinity of 9 million acres, leaving a net saving of about as much. This is in terms of average grain-crops acres in the wheat areas. As a practical matter, if land is saved it will be foremost from among low-yielding lands; thus even more acres would be saved but acres of lower quality. They would also be among the more erosion prone lands which would be better used as pasture or as forest. It is true that saving land does not save all production inputs to the same extent—fertilizers, especially, are used in greater quantities on high yielding crops such as corn and sorghum. But saving land undoubtedly saves fuel, and machinery depreciation, for field operations and somewhat more so when the land saved is in large areas of low fertile land.

Of the wheat harvest, about one-third is used for food in the United States. The rest is mainly exported, some minor amounts used as livestock feed (other than bran). Thus, if all wheat bread in this country were dark, this would save upwards of 3 million acres annually. This still does not regard what customers in other countries do. Assuming we would not go to only dark bread, we can still say that every ten percent of the bread that is shifted from white to all-dark (whole wheat altogether) would save on the order of 300 thousand acres which would be freed up for other production or for conservation use, or both. Our current very small use of dark flour saves only 30,000 acres, in comparison with a situation where there were no dark bread at all.

The bread story is in fact the least part of waste in the food system. In its limited way, it already shows how consumer welfare is manipulated in the interest of suppliers at all levels, from farmers (and their suppliers) to millers, bakers, and food retailers. The classical case of social waste in food is in margarine versus butter.

THE FAT OF THE LAND

Let us begin with the Iowa margarine scandal. In 1943, at the height of World War II and amid shortages and rationings, scientists in Ames had put out an extension publication which explained to the public that margarine is fully as nourishing and wholesome as butter; and of course it is much cheaper—it cost about half as much as butter at that time already. Under pressure from farming interests, the Iowa Agricultural Experiment Station withdrew the publication and thus ceased its effort to enlighten the public. In the storm that followed, numerous academics at Iowa State College of Agriculture resigned and went to employment elsewhere. One of these was T. W. Schultz, one of the nation's leading agricultural economists who many years later won the Nobel Prize in Economics.

There have been many more skirmishes in the struggle of farming interests to protect the market for butter. The State of Wisconsin held out until a few years ago in a deliberate policy of denying margarine free competition with butter. Such policies caused some delay but could not at length prevent the increasing prevalence of vegetable fats over butter and other animal fats in daily food consumption. Delay it they did, causing social waste while the delays lasted.

The statistics show food fats as a relatively slow-changing group of commodities in the United States. From the early 1930's to recent years, the total of the commodity group doubled in volume, even as the population grew by about 80 percent. Thus, per-capita consumption of food fats rose only moderately. Milk and milkfat both remained nearly unchanged over the same period, hence their per-capita amount fell a great deal. Table fat (butter and margarine together) rose by only one-tenth over the same half century. Other edible fats increased much more, thus the salad oils and cheese. But the composition of table fat changed drastically: in 1931, margarine was less than one-tenth of the total; it came to the same volume as butter in the late 1950's, and by the late 1970's, margarine had risen to more than 70 percent of the table fat. Now it outweighs butter in a ratio that is close to 3:1. At the same time the price difference has grown even wider, margarine is now a good deal cheaper than half the price of butter. Quality of margarine has risen continuously and there is now no doubt that margarine is fully as valuable as butter. When some people continue to prefer butter, this is hard to explain except by the force of habit.

Although the volume of butter, marketed as table fat, is now not much more than one-third of what it was 50 years ago, yet milk and butterfat have remained at about the same total volume in the country. The difference, by and large, has been absorbed by cheese, a group of foods which expanded vigorously in American production and diet. It is also an item of increasing net imports, so there should be room for some import substitution. The recent give-away of government held cheese produced under price support points to a complicated conflict.

In the total food fat supply of the United States, commodities other than direct table fat have increased a great deal. Like margarine, most of the increase (in salad oils, cooking oils, baking fat, etc.) has come from vegetable oils, foremost (by a long stretch) soybean oil.

Dairy farming occupies a good deal of land in the United States. Like milk production, dairy-farm land has changed but little in the last five decades. Dairy farms (those where milk production is the principal enterprise) cover about 100 million acres, of which 35–40 million acres are cropland. In addition, dairy farms also buy some processed feed which has been grown on land in other farms (mainly cash-grain farms). In recent time, this feed purchased by dairy farmers has been about 8 million tons a year and can be estimated to have been grown on about 3 million acres of cropland. This cropland used "indirectly" for dairy farming may have increased somewhat in recent years, to offset some slight decline in cropland on the dairy farms themselves.

Progress in dairy farming has been mainly by raising the yield of milk per cow, and by increasing the efficiency of dairy-farm workers so they can handle more cows each. Milk production per unit of labor has risen a great deal, and the relative price of milk (how much of a consumer's wages are needed to buy a given quantity of milk) has fallen in proportion. But the output of milk per unit of land area has not changed much, not even when we look only at the cropland used for dairy farming. This is in contrast to the crops that produce vegetable fat. Soybeans, especially, have meant a great increase in amount of fat produced per unit of cropland used for such crops.

All milk fat (whether used as butter, cheese, whole milk, or whatnot) is about 4½ billion pounds, meaning 45 pounds per acre of all dairy land or somewhat more than 100 pounds per acre of cropland in dairy farms. Less than one-fifth of all milk fat is now marketed as butter. Since the 1930's butter has declined by two-thirds while margarine has risen tenfold and vegetable shortening nearly fourfold. If we were to supply all the table and cooking fat from butter in the same proportion to vegetable fats as fifty years ago, we would need to use almost twice as much land for dairy farming as compared to what is used now. If butter were to have maintained its market quantity unchanged even while cheese rose as it did, this would have necessitated one-third more dairy land than now—say, 30–35 million acres more, of which 12–14 million acres would have to be cropland.

Expansion of oilseeds took much less land. Soybeans, for instance, yielding 30 bushels (1800 pounds) per acre, and 18 percent oil in the beans, yield 300–350 pounds of fat per acre. Now, of course, both milk and soybeans contain other food besides fat. In both products, the fat and the non-fat components represent about half of the value, so the fat yield per acre remains comparable. Even though soybeans are generally grown on better land than that used for dairy farming, the resource saving through margarine and other vegetable fats is very large. It would be even larger if the non-fat part of the oilseed were used directly as human food, more than happens now. It can be done by meat substitutes but also, and more directly, by milk substitutes.

Artificial milk from soy protein is already an accomplished fact, but industry and commerce are hesitant to use it. To some extent artificial milk has begun to be used in ice cream. Other than that, one finds here and there in very well stocked groceries some articles of artificial milk and products based on it, recommended for people whose health does not allow them to consume natural milk.

This is timid indeed, for those in the know agree that most kinds of cheese can be duplicated from artificial milk, and at much lower cost than that for cheese made from natural milk. As far as the cheese is concerned, the difference would be less than for fluid milk, for even milk-based cheese is a product of chemical transformation—even natural milk is merely a raw material. Publications from the USDA sometimes refer to artificial cheese as a possible threat to dairy farming which might slow down progress otherwise expected from various improvements, such as those of the biological stock of dairy cattle. No one seems willing to admit that, if things are allowed to move by the logic of technology and economics, the milk cow, within twenty or thirty years, will be as obsolete as the draft horse. To the contrary, we already see advertising campaigns purporting to "prove" that natural milk is so good that nothing synthetic can replace either it or the products made from it. Apparently we are going to see the anti-margarine campaign all over again. Depending on how successful the resistance against synthetic milk products turns out to be, the social waste can be very large—the waste in gains foregone for a generation of Americans who might get their food cheaper and at less cost in scarce resources.

THE MEAT OF THE PROBLEM

Most of the farmland in the United States produces meat. This is true not only of the 600 million acres classified as pastures, and the additional large areas dubbed "woodland pastured". It is true also for half of the cropland.

The statistics show that livestock and poultry eat about 500 million tons (short tons, of 2000 pounds or 907 kilograms) of feed annually. Of this, some 180–185 million tons were concentrates in recent years and the rest roughage. The latter consists of pasture grass (over 200 million tons) and harvested roughage such as hay, silage and straw, which amounted to some 80–90 million tons. The concentrates are just about the equivalent of the annual harvest of cereal grains minus that part which is exported. The exports were about one-third of the grain crops. Domestic consumption, which took two-thirds, goes directly into human food (such as bread, etc.) only to a minor extent. Most of the grains become livestock feed. Livestock also eat large parts of other crops, above all the non-fat parts of soybeans and other oilseeds. For simplicity we will summarize by saying that feed concentrates fed to livestock in the United States are roughly equal to the two-thirds of the cereal grain harvest which are not exported.

Grain crops occupy about 160 to 175 million acres a year, of the 360 million acres or so which were used for crop production in recent years. Thus feed concentrates lay claim to the output of some 100–120 million acres of grain crops or their equivalent in oilseeds etc., or nearly one-third of our cropland. And this is to a large extent the better cropland, as corn and soybeans dominate on the high productive lands of the Midwest. Hay crops are harvested from some 60 million acres a year, and thus stockfeed occupies half of the country's cropland resources.

Foremost among the livestock is cattle, of which four-fifths are beef animals and one-fifth dairy cattle. Cattle consumes nearly all of the roughages; sheep are a minor enterprise in this country. Dairy pastures, as we already discussed, are obviously a minor portion of all pastures, most of which thus go into producing beef. In factory mixed feed concentrates, dairy cattle take a somewhat larger share than do beef cattle. But all factory mixed feeds are not much more than one-fourth of all feed concentrates, the rest being unprocessed grain when it enters the livestock industry. The largest consumer of factory mixed feeds are the poultry farms. Next come the hog farms, but many of them process their own mixed feed.

Meat consumption in the United States is not the highest in the world. Argentina, for instance, is far ahead of us there. But meat consumption in this country is without any doubt greater than is needed for sound and sufficient nutrition. In recent years Americans on the average consumed 180 pounds of red meat per year plus 55–60 pounds of poultry meat (chickens and turkeys), and close to 300 eggs. Red meat rose from 160 pounds per year around 1960 to 190 pounds a few years ago; it has declined somewhat in recent years. Poultry consumption also rose since 1960 and now appears steady, while eggs are declining slowly. Of the red meat, over two-thirds are beef and veal—currently somewhat declining. Close to one-third is pork which is holding steady with some cyclical variation. Mutton (lamb) is a small part of the U.S. meat supply.

In the total food budget of American households, meat is a substantial portion and it would seem an obvious target for economizing. Apart from the possibility of eating less meat and more of conventional vegetable foods, we now also have the offering of artificial meat substitutes made from the protein in soybeans and other crops. The analogy with margarine is incomplete because these meat "analogs" are as yet far from replacing whole steaks. What they can substitute for, as of now, is the meat in many processed dishes such as soups, stews, and meatballs or hamburgers. Even in these, the indications at present are that vegetable protein could replace some fraction, such as one-fourth, rather than the whole meat dish. Even so, the resource saving would be sustantial if the "analogs" were accepted across the board. There are also some complete dishes, such as sausages or imitation bacon which can be made entirely from artificial meat. A few years ago, the USDA conducted a test marketing project in a medium sized city (Fort Wayne, Indiana). Among the findings was that, in the form in which the bacon is served on the platter (fully cooked, ready to eat) artificial bacon had required one-tenth as much land as the same quantity of natural bacon strips. For beef meat, the proportion would be closer to one-in-twenty.

It is of course evident that the whole resource saving which will be possible through vegetable based meat substitutes can not be cashed in all at once, just because the technology has been developed. Some food processing industries have invested vigorously in research and product development toward meat substitutes and other high-protein foods from vegetable sources. So have some academic institutions—thus with synthetic milk. Consumer acceptance will no doubt take some time, but does it have to take as long as it now takes? Marketing progress appears to be at a snail's pace, much slower than the advance of technology.

This lag between invention and use entails a good deal of social waste. We do not mean consumers' reluctance which we have to accept as long as it is genuine and spontaneous. No, social waste comes from the fact that the meat interests—beginning with farmers and ranchers, and continuing through the meat packing establishment and into retail—do what they can to retard and to frustrate the movement toward meat substitutes, just as dairy interests did against margarine and still do against synthetic substitutes for milk and cheese. The USDA, after a brief departure into test marketing and other tentative promoting of meat substitutes a few years ago, has retreated into positions which defend natural meat. The rationale used is the statement that natural meat is what consumers want, period. The immediate line of defense was to increase research and extension aimed at producing leaner meat. The extreme fat of "marbled beef" was found not be as popular as previous meat trade appeared to show. More red meat and less animal fat might be healthier and less wasteful of feed resources. But this defense of natural meat also means an unwillingness, on the part of the USDA as well as of the meat industries, to let consumer demand take its own unrestrained course.

The official line about consumer demand assumes it to be essentially free from commercial manipulation. This is seldom entirely true. A case in point is in this country's meat imports. Yes, despite all the surplus of agricultural production (of which feed crops are the bulk), the United States does import meat. The difference between imports and exports of meat adds another five per cent to meat consumption in this country. When the meat industry is so keen at defending its markets, why do they tolerate such imports? The answer usually given is that imported beef, mainly from Mexico and Australia, is a different commodity from U.S. corn finished beef. The imports come from "scrub cattle", nondescript beef animals fed almost entirely on pasture, and this meat is not served as steaks in this country but goes chiefly into hamburgers which thereby can be made cheaper. Indirectly, we are told, this serves the domestic meat interests because cheap hamburgers give young Americans a habit of eating beef meat, which would prepare them for a lifetime of steaks when they mature into higher incomes. Thus the public's demand for meat is not entirely a spontaneous growth from the depth of the people's soul. It is in part an artificial product of marketing, carefully nurtured for the purpose of maximizing the eventual demand for meat.

The least one could expect from the USDA, as guardian of the whole national interest in regard to food and agriculture, would be neutrality toward honest competition for the consumers' expenditures. If the artificial meats (and other high-protein foods of vegetable origin, including soy milk) were given a completely even break, we could already now save considerable resources needlessly invested in domestic meat consumption. The resource saving would soon equal that from margarine and eventually become much larger. Land freed from meat production would not only make land available for other production whether food for export (including foreign aid) or in non-food products at home such as wool, fuel, or timber. It would also save machine fuel, fertilizers and factory resources—in machine building and in feed processing, for instance. There could also be some switch toward growing meat directly on pastures—if grass fed cattle can be imported, for hamburgers, why can not some such production take place at home too?

The fuel saving can not be disregarded lightly. American agriculture is not a particularly energy intensive sector, not as the American economy goes. But the U.S. economy is the most energy intensive in the world, and as the next chapter will show, energy savings will have to be sought at all levels where they are at all possible.

Chapter 3
Money to Burn: Oil Waste in America

High consumption of petroleum in this country has long been taken for granted, and has even been hailed as the epitome of prosperity. Little thought was given to the questions of how long this could last or how little is really gained by wasting oil at the prodigious rate which has become customary. The following two chapters will argue that oil waste has led to many negative consequences. The country would have been better off—in many respects—if the waste had been curbed long ago. For now, let us first lay down just how high the level of oil consumption has been and still is, and then show some of the general consequences of this waste for today's economy, including the recently quite frequent recessions.

FUEL USE IN THE UNITED STATES AND IN OTHER COUNTRIES

How wasteful America is with oil and other energy sources can best be shown by comparing it with other countries. Most of the world is much more economical in the use of energy. This will tell us something about how much energy might be saved in this country. The savings made to date—since the first oil price crisis of 1973–74—are quite modest. The remaining scope for saving of energy—of oil, particularly—should be many times larger in the United States than has been achieved.

How small these savings have been is remarkable. The impact of higher energy prices, both 1973–74 and 1979–81, was particularly severe on this country because of its high level of energy consumption. Data from the United Nations, expressing energy use as kilograms per capita of coal-equivalent energy, show the people of the United States consuming the equivalent of 11,500 kilograms of coal per person in 1973, still 11,200 in 1979, and 10,400 in 1980. Thus the decline was by less than one-tenth, at the depth of a recession. The people of France consumed 4,300 kilograms of coal-equivalent energy per person in 1980, and they have a real per-capita national income which is 80 percent of that in the United States. The West Germans, with an income level close to that of France, consumed 5,700 kilograms per person, the Japanese 3,700, and the people of the Soviet Union 5,600.

The comparison becomes even more striking when we look at motor gasoline. People in the United States consumed 1,362 kilograms per person in 1973, even a little more in the late 1970's, and still 1,244 in 1980, a decline proportionately smaller than that of all energy. Consumption of gasoline in 1980 was 300 kilos per person in France, 200 in Japan and 250 in the USSR.

The position of the United States remains exceptional even when we take into account differences in real per-capita incomes. Recently, we have been given national income figures that can be compared between countries better than before. This is through the World Bank project on international comparisons of national product. According to such data, the United States in 1973 consumed 1.86 kilograms of coal-equivalent energy per dollar's worth of national product. France consumed half of that, West Germany two-thirds, for each dollar's worth of internationally comparable national product. Of the European countries, only the United Kingdom came relatively close to the U.S consumption level, with 1.40 kilos per dollar's worth of national income. But the U.K. has a slow-growing economy with problems even more severe than our own, so we should not cite their case in our favor. It is possible that the Soviet Union may rival the United States in energy consumption per unit of real national product, but this is hard to prove because the systems of national accounting are different. But this comparison would be even less in our favor than that with the United Kingdom, because the Soviet economy is very wasteful of resources and it now has enormous problems of low and sluggish productivity.

Most of the difference in energy consumption, when America is compared with other industrialized countries, comes from motor gasoline. When that is taken out of the picture, the remaining difference in energy consumption per unit of national product—the difference in energy forms other than motor gasoline—is much smaller. Then the United States consumption is only one-and-two-thirds of that of France or Japan, only one-fourth ahead of West Germany, and less than one-tenth ahead of the United Kingdom.

CONSUMPTION VERSUS CAPITAL FORMATION

The exceptionally high level of gasoline use in the United States points to private consumption as a main source of difference in energy use as compared with other industrial countries. The World Bank study on comparable national product throws some light on this. In 1973, France, West Germany and Japan used between 55 and 60 percent of their national product for private consumption, the United States over two-thirds (almost 68 percent). The difference was all in two sectors: transportation and housing. In the United States these sectors took over one-third of all private consumption, or nearly one-fourth of the national product. In the other three countries, the same two sectors absorbed relatively only half as much as in the United States, Other private consumption (other than transportation and housing) took about the same share of national product in all four countries. By contrast, capital formation received a much larger share of the national product in France, Germany and Japan than in the United States. Despite their lower level of real national product per person, all three countries invested a good deal more—even in absolute terms—per person than the United States.

Again, the high level of private consumption in the United States is rivalled only by that of the United Kingdom, another slow growing economy with insufficient capital formation. France, Germany and Japan all showed the source of their economic success in much higher rates of investment which are possible when private consumption claims a lesser share of national product.

So, the over-weight of private consumption in the United States is concentrated in the housing and transportation sectors. This is serious, for two reasons. First, these sectors are very energy intensive and are responsible for most if not all of the differences in energy intensity as compared with the fast-growing industrial countries. Second, both sectors are slow moving, hard to change. Both sectors also create other problems besides high consumption of energy and capital, as we shall discuss in the following two chapters.

The high energy intensity of transportation is well known. In direct account, transportation in the United States consumes about 26 percent of all commercial energy. When indirect energy (utilized through the "backward linkages" in other sectors of the economy) of the transportation complex is included, then the transportation sector absorbs about 45–46 percent of the whole national energy budget. Private cars take about two-thirds of the transportation total, or 30 percent of all the nation's energy. It may in fact be more, because truck transportation partly serves the car system by hauling petroleum and cars en route to market.

Space heating and cooling is another large energy consuming sector. Most of this is residential—a form of consumption. In 1978–79, residential use of natural gas, fuel oil, and electricity amounted to 13½ percent of all commercial energy in the country. Including the energy cost of supplying the gas, the fuel oil, and the electricity, the bill climbs to nearly one-fourth of the country's energy budget. Electricity in residential use is of course not all for air conditioning and heating, but use of other electricity operated gadgets is also in some degree related to the size of the houses. Moreover, the figures cited do not include the energy used in backward linkages other than those of the energy system itself. Building and maintaining the housing inventory, including its furnaces, windows, insulation etc.—all of these also consume energy. It is therefore no exaggeration to say that housing alone takes at least one-fifth of all commercial energy in the United States. Together with private transportation this comes to half or more of the total national energy budget; household appliances absorb another 5–10 percent. The two sectors we are discussing make up one-third of private consumption by dollar value, or barely one-fourth of the national product or expenditure. Other private consumption in the United States absorbs no more of the national product than in other countries, and proportionately not much more energy either.

The only other sector where the United States deviates sharply from other industrial countries of the free world is in government expenditures for commodities, that is mainly for defense hardware. The World Bank national product figures (from the international comparison project) for 1973 show the United States using 6 percent of its national product for government procurements. Germany, France and Japan all used half or less than half as much of their national product for the same type of purpose. The consequences we shall explore in a later chapter. At this point we must remember that the defense sector is a sinkhole for resources. It has no forward linkages into other production as has civilian use of heavy investment goods similar to those of the weapons systems. The conjunction of energy intensive and materials intensive high defense needs with a high level of private consumption in energy intensive transportation and housing—this combination certainly should have made us expect a heavier impact from rising energy prices in this country than anywhere else in the world. So far, not much of this kind of insight has been brought to bear on the debate about our economic difficulties.

OIL CRISIS, INFLATION, AND RECESSION

Let us recall some essential facts of recent years about the supply and price of petroleum and other energy sources. Before 1973, primary energy cost the United States economy about 3 percent of its national product. It had been of that magnitude—with variations—for many years, at least since the turn of the century. In the 1950's and 1960's, the unit cost of energy was slightly falling because of the increasing role of natural gas which was then very inexpensive.

Following the first OPEC oil price increases of 1973-74, other energy prices also went up. Despite some decline in the real price of oil after 1974 (because of inflation), the cost of all energy to the American economy in the late 1970's has risen to about 6 percent of the national product. The second round of oil price increases in 1979-80, and the decontrol of domestic oil prices (by stages, from September 1976 through January 1981) brought the entire energy bill to the level of 12 percent of the national product by 1981. Oil glut and falling gasoline prices at retail for a while masked the longer-term trend, but those tendencies have now run their course; gasoline prices have again risen to almost their former level in current terms even as inflation has abated. The new high level of energy costs to the economy will be further bolstered by de-control of natural-gas prices. For oil, medium-term forecasts from the Department of Energy (early 1980's) expect rising prices in the 1990's, to about twice the current level in constant dollars.

The primary connection between oil prices, inflation and recession is easy to demonstrate. No matter how the statistics are presented, it is clear that each of the two large oil price increases was followed by rising inflation, falling national product, and rising unemployment. In between, in the years 1975–78 which were years of economic recovery, oil prices were falling slightly, normal economic expansion resumed, inflation was slower and unemployment went down.

When a new phenomenon follows upon a new event, some connection should have been suspected from the start. Yet many economists appeared bewildered because "stagflation" (as the new combination of inflation and economic stagnation was dubbed) did not seem to fit received theory. The second wave of oil price increases and of "stagflation" followed the pattern of the first one, and still the lesson was hard to learn. The recent reduction in the rate of inflation (late 1981 to end of 1983) does not contradict the conclusion about "stagflation"'s origin in oil prices, for the remedy applied in 1981 and 1982, in record-high real interest rates, was strong enough to submerge the oil price effect while depressing both investment, consumption, and employment.

Decontrol of domestic crude oil prices was de facto accomplished, for the most part, by the end of 1980.[1] It can of course be argued that decontrol may have been accelerated by devious means, as by some oil operators reporting old oil as new, but that does not affect the conclusion about the timing of actual decontrol which is based on a data source close to the refinery industry.

What bewildered many economists was the connection between cost-push inflation and recession. Inflation by costs pushing prices upward was supposed to happen only in times of strong economic expansion. Periods of economic contraction should have less cost-push and less inflation. This misunderstanding came about because previously, costs pushing prices upward had been mainly the costs of labor which would tend upward under full employment. Rising labor costs are a normal—in fact a necessary—component of sustained economic expansion, for without higher wage incomes of workers there will at length not be enough demand for the output of expanding industry. Rising labor costs

---

1. The part decontrolled in late January 1981 (instead of September of the same year as previously envisaged) was minor.

translate into rising effective demand for the whole gamut of consumer goods, including consumers' durables and housing.

With a natural resource such as energy rising in cost, the effect should have been expected to be quite different. It should have been expected, but there had not been much experience of this—natural resources had been falling in cost for a long time due to improving technology. When natural resources rise in price, the increasing purchasing power of the resource owners (those owning oil and gas fields, for instance) does not accrue to the general public in the same way as increased wages do, for the resource owners are much fewer than the workers. To the extent that the resource owners are foreign, that part of the rising cost goes abroad, and the effects on the U.S. economy are then quite different from those of domestic consumer demand. To the extent that the resource owners are domestic, such as U.S. oil companies, they will invest a large part of the proceeds from increased revenue into continued production of the resource. This was in fact a large part of the argument in favor of oil price decontrol. But the drilling boom of 1980–81, now long over, did not stimulate the economy as a whole. It stimulated only certain sectors, such as suppliers of heavy equipment, and these sectors are capital intensive and energy intensive and they generate less employment (in relation to size of their orders) than do most other sectors. The same is true of the oil industry itself and of its drilling boom. Oil employs only small numbers of high paid people; the oil industry is "expertise intensive" as well as capital intensive and energy intensive. In petroleum and electricity, the amount of capital per worker is from six to seven times as much as the average in U.S. manufacturing as a whole. The more capital there is per worker, the higher paid must the workers be, to ensure the right level of competence in handling all that expensive equipment. This means that with the oil drilling boom, the oil-and-gas complex laid claim to a widening share of the country's resources in capital and skilled manpower, thus dampening expansion outside the energy industries and their suppliers.

Between the two "stagflation" episodes there was this difference, however: In 1973–74, most of the price pressure came from abroad. It bore down most directly on foreign exchange, which also led to some increase in foreign-owned investments in the

United States. Since 1979, oil imports have declined in volume if not in cost. The rise in domestic oil prices has been relatively greater than the rise in import prices, and this rise in domestic prices is now projected on a larger volume of oil because all domestic oil has become high priced. The economic strain is therefore now more directly on the domestic capital market.

OIL AND INVESTMENT

How much real investment that goes into oil and other energy business depends on statistical definitions; the several data sources are not easy to compare. Whichever way the evidence is turned around, however, one thing remains certain: capital spending for oil and other energy sources has risen to record levels in recent years. One set of data, released in 1981, showed capital spending by the oil sector (in the large sense, including refining, petrochemicals, and coal mines owned by oil companies) more than doubling (in current terms) from 1979 to 1982. For oil production alone, which took almost half of the total, the rate of expansion was nearly as large—more than a doubling—and more sustained into the projections for 1982. The increased capital spending for petroleum production, refining, marketing etc. was large enough to displace investment in other sectors of the economy to a substantial degree. This happened at the same time as the ever larger Federal budget deficits make the national government also lay claim to a larger and larger share of the nation's savings and resources.

Another set of data, published by the Petroleum Economist of London, showed oil investment in the United States, in constant prices, rising faster than the growth of the national economy over the decade 1980–1990. Oil and gas were assumed to grow the most.

The energy sectors are not only capital intensive and expertise intensive. They are also energy intensive, and increasingly so. Data from the Census of Mineral Industries show that energy consumption in the oil and gas fields, per unit of oil and gas produced, doubled between 1967 and 1977. No doubt this trend has continued and probably it has accelerated. Extraction of heavy oil in California, for instance, is reported to consume a large part of its own output to make steam for its own activity, to release more heavy oil so it can be pumped. The recent drilling boom was a disappointment to those who expected energy independence from domestic oil. The boom produced little results beyond slowing down the continuing downtrend in domestic oil production. Many small wells have been drilled in old oilfields, but the great majority of the holes are dry. There have been no major new finds in the United States recently—either offshore, in the mountains, or elsewhere. Domestic oil production has just been holding steady for some time but informed analysts expect it soon to begin going down by one or two percent per year. The gamble of offshore drilling goes on in some places, but the costs are very high.

When the pressure of the energy sectors on the capital resources of the country is so strong, we must raise the question why the economy is and continues to be so energy intensive. We must find out what might have been done about all this—and why it was not done.

TIME TRENDS IN THE UNITED STATES

This brings us to the trends in spending for housing and transportation. Long-term statistics show these energy intensive sectors of private spending to be gradually gaining ground. Together they took about 18 to 20 percent of the national product from 1929 to 1965. In the same span of time, other private spending fell from 55 percent to 45 percent of the national product. In other words, total private spending fell (relatively), but the reduction was in the less energy intensive sectors. Since 1970, transportation and housing have risen from 19 percent of the GNP to over 22 percent, that is to an unprecedented high. This was at the same time as all private spending rose only slightly, from 63 percent to 64 percent of the GNP, and private spending other than for transportation and housing fell from 44 percent to 41 percent of the GNP. As a consequence, the share of transportation and housing in all private consumer spending rose from 26 percent in 1929, to 30 percent in 1970 and to 35 percent in 1980–81.

The decline in the percentage of national product going to private consumer spending, and of consumption other than for transportation and housing is, of course, minor compared with the general rise in affluence. From 1940 to 1980, the American economy quadrupled in size, and real per-capita national product rose more than threefold. All consumption rose vigorously, the energy intensive sectors much more so than other kinds of consumption. The cumulative effect is easy to overlook in retrospect. For decades, oil consumption in this country rose at such a rate that half of the historical (cumulative) total was in the last ten years; in other words, the historical total doubled every ten years. Thus oil consumption increased at a rate far in excess of the rate of growth of the economy.

The rise in the share of the energy intensive transportation and housing sectors we discussed in current terms. In constant prices, the rise has been less, but whatever gains there have been in "conservation" (more efficient use of energy) are more than offset by price increases in recent years. Current prices are relevant here because these are the terms in which the economy is being strained. The rising level of outlays for the energy intensive kinds of consumption means less money (and fewer real resources) available for the less energy intensive ones such as health care and other labor intensive services. Correspondingly more of all business receipts will be used for investment in the capital-, energy-, and expertise-intensive energy sectors.

The failure of the energy intensive sectors of consumption to contract when prices rose means, in the parlance of economics, that price elasticities of demand are low at the consumer (or, end-use) level. For transportation and housing in the United States, the causes of these low elasticities are not hard to find. Housing is a fixed-investment sector receiving public subsidy by means of tax deduction for mortgage interest. Once the bulk of the housing inventory has been built, it has to be operated and maintained by heating etc., else much of it would deteriorate by attrition. Much of this expense is captive. Continued construction of more and more spatious housing is both encouraged by the tax system and forced along by the rigidities of the transportation system. Blueprints for more energy efficient housing are now available, but mostly these energy saving features are omitted in actual construction to cut down immediate costs. Short-term economizing by consumers thus gets in the way of long-term rationality.

The transportation system, as we shall see in some detail in the next chapter, is in turn captive partly because of the spatious layout of most of the housing system and partly because a more economic one, such as efficient mass transit, gets muscled out by the lavish use of private cars. Again, individuals tend to count costs in the short run. Immediate outlays for gasoline are compared with bus ticket prices, leaving out the total cost of car operation including its medium-term overhead.

EFFECTS ON THE WORLD OF UNITED STATES CONSUMPTION HABITS

The discussion above shows that American consumption habits are directly responsible for the country's import demand for petroleum. If this country had been as economical in the use of fuel as most of Europe, for instance, we would not need to import any oil. The reserves in the ground would then also have been larger than they are now, and the time in which to develop substitute fuels could have been longer.

American consumption habits are also responsible for the whole foreign policy syndrome of recent years. The entire web of Middle East politics depends on this one factor. Without this unnecessary import demand, the United States would have had a much freer hand to pursue its foreign policy according to essential criteria of international order. There would then also be much less policy pressure on other countries, specifically western Europe and Japan. Pressures on them would also have had less leverage on the foreign policy of the United States.

This extends to the pricing of oil in international trade. High petroleum prices prompted by the demand in the United States have accelerated inflation not only in this country but also world wide. The energy problem in Europe could have been much less urgent if the U.S. did not import oil. Even the need for a gas pipeline from the Soviet Union to Europe might have had less attraction, and its potential for Soviet leverage on Europe could also have been less, if the United States were living within its own means in regard to energy. How sharply U.S. demand has impinged upon the world is particularly clear when we dwell upon the OPEC and how it gained its position of power.

OPEC AND UNITED STATES OIL INTERESTS

It can be argued quite plausibly that the OPEC is a creature of the U.S. oil majors. Having encouraged the rapid depletion of domestic oil resources, in the interest of their own high level of income, the oil majors understood very well that their position within the United States would be strengthened by higher import prices.

OPEC went into action for high prices precisely at the juncture when the situation in the United States began to invite this, that is, when imports had become a large part of this country's oil supply, and when the U.S. consumption habits had become deeply enough entrenched so they would not change much because of higher prices. From one-tenth in the mid-fifties, U.S. net oil imports had risen to one-fourth of total domestic oil consumption by 1970 and to almost 40 percent in 1973. The invitation to interfere was getting more tempting every year.

Tempting also to the oil majors. They not only own most of the domestic oil fields, they also do most of the importing. OPEC not only brought them higher prices for domestic oil but also larger profits from their import business.

True to their basic motivation, the oil industry also does its share to play down both "conservation" (more economic use of energy) and the search for alternative sources to replace oil and gas. In this drive to prolong the country's dependency on oil, they have powerful allies in the automotive complex, the highway lobby, and the construction industry.

Until recently, it appeared that OPEC oil prices were geared to the objective of not encouraging the growth of substitute fuel industries in the United States. By thus abetting our wasteful consumption habits, OPEC and the oil majors in concert were also prolonging the whole foreign-policy syndrome that follows from dependency on imported oil.

How did the United States economy get stuck in such a destructive pattern of resource use? The 1950's appear as a crossroad.

CHOICES OF THE 1950's AND THE 1980's

U.S. statistics show the 1950's were a period in which energy intensive private consumption gained a larger share in national product than before. Important decisions were taken which rendered the current system less avoidable than it might otherwise have been.

Following experiences of World War II, the Truman administration had to some extent reflected on resource scarcity, not the least for its potential strategic consequences. An inquiry was started (the

Paley Commission), and experimental Research-and-Development plants for synthetic fuels were financed by the Federal government. In 1953, the incoming Republican administration put a virtual stop to all this. The Paley Commission's report, which had just come out, was shelved—the decision was taken not to act on its recommendations. Three experimental plants for synthetic fuels (two using coal and one processing oil shale) were scrapped, their buildings either torn down or turned over to the Army for warehousing.

This was at the same time that South Africa, with resources a small fraction of those of the United States, went ahead with their oil-from coal project, an industry where they now have the only full-scale activity in the world. At the time, it was already known that domestic petroleum in continental United States would become scarce and eventually run out, in a matter of decades. One expert predicted that U.S. oil extraction would peak in the time span 1968–71; it actually did so in 1970. So strong was the force of wishful thinking that even oil executives had difficulty following the logic of Hubbert's prediction. Subsequent studies have confirmed the low likelihood of large new oil discoveries in the United States.

Inability, or unwillingness, to gauge the future decline of oil in the United States was one factor in the energy optimism of the 1950's. Another was exaggerated faith in nuclear power. "Peaceful uses of the atom", that slogan was an important political tenet of a regime which hoped to base national security on nuclear weapons. The immense destructive power of such weapons might be less repulsive if the spinoff in civilian economic benefits were large. Nuclear powered electricity would be "too cheap to meter", so the myth ran. What an illusion that was has become clear only gradually. Some unpleasant discoveries may yet be to come, not only as to the cost of stashing away the nuclear debris from the power stations but also in the cost of de-commissioning old nuclear plants; this has not yet begun but it is likely to be an expensive affair. Illusion it was, the myth of cheap nuclear power, but the consequences are still with us.

The legacy of the 1950's is cast in concrete in the over-large system of superhighways and the too great dependence on trucks and cars. The 1960's largely continued on the momentum set in motion in the 1950's. The oil crisis of 1973–74 stirred a debate which attempted to include both technical efficiency and system change. The "Project Independence" of the Nixon administration emphasized mainly production. So did, in fact, also the Department of Energy under the Carter administration. There were some attempts at making the system in place more efficient, but to systematic change there was little more than lip service.

The policies now in effect are essentially an attempt at reverting to those of the 1950's, with very little regard for the realities of scarce natural resources. Leading circles in Washington continue to insist on positions set forth in the 1980 election campaign, that market mechanisms will solve our economic problems, including that of energy, if they are only left free to operate without political interference. In thus treating the market as if it were a force of nature, these people appear to overlook the fact that any society always operates under some set of institutions which are not necessarily what current market forces would choose if they had an entirely free choice. Rather, these institutions (reflections of past policy decisions) in many ways determine how current markets may function. This applies very much to energy use in the United States which reflects policies and attitudes of a time when energy was no perceptible problem—specifically the 1950's and the mistakes in long-term resource use which were taken at that time.

Current U.S. policy is especially improvident in that it makes very little provision for replacement energy sources to be on hand when oil and gas begin to run out. We have no reason to expect that oil will always be available for import as it is now. Many of the present oil exporting countries are likely to begin reducing their exports around 1990 (give or take a year or two). This is because their own industry and its need for fuel is growing, and the time will come when they have to keep their remaining oil supplies for themselves. Domestic oil will increasingly be used up by the oil industry itself, leaving less and less of its output for the rest of the economy. There are already (Fall 1983) signs that U.S. oil imports will begin increasing again. If economic recovery is strong, increased oil imports are a foregone conclusion. The same follows both from rising prices of natural gas and from the expected decline in U.S. domestic oil production. In consequence, oil prices will resume their upward trend.

Lack of foresight was particularly evident in the rhetoric of the Republican election campaign in 1980. We were told that the United States is an oil-rich nation, a patently incorrect assessment of the situation. The lack of success in the drilling boom of 1980–81 should now have informed us otherwise, but no policy shift is in sight—not even to acknowledge, or do something about, the sharply increased real costs of domestic oil.

The belief that fuel will always be available at some price seems to disregard the fact that there can be fuel prices that would break the back of any economic system. The share of the energy complex in the national product can not be allowed to rise indefinitely. We may in fact be close to a limit which could not be tolerated.

In the past, America was incredibly lucky. Petroleum, and later natural gas, became available in quantities which initially were far greater than anyone had any use for, and the costs of extraction were trivial compared to the marginal product generated by putting those energy sources to work. These initial quantities, and subsequent major finds, were not the result of anyone's ingenuity, but of geological happenstances million of years ago.

Such lucky stumbling into riches is no longer likely. Our most recent experience shows that now the marginal cost for oil is very high and may be rising toward intolerable levels. When current policy merely encourages the oil operators to go on drilling without regard for the cost to the national economy, it is clearly steering the country toward very hard times in the medium-term future. They are also maintaining and eventually worsening the foreign-policy consequences of the oil waste. The risks and uncertainties of developing replacement resources are generally not acceptable to private industry. Without major public support, this essential task will be left undone for the time being and possibly until it is too late.

ROOTS OF IMPROVIDENCE

The picture of the United States eroding essential resources and shifting a good deal of the economic damage "downstream" to other countries, makes us ask what are the mechanisms behind such lack of foresight and responsibility.

The energy situation we are in since 1973 could and should have been anticipated in the 1950's; the information was already at hand. Some warning voices were heard but they were deliberately ignored. Long-term analysis would have shown that in social account, the discounted value of future oil supplies was already a good deal higher than was reflected in the market prices then being paid for oil products. Since individuals and firms are not expected to take on problems of this magnitude, the national government should have done so. It could have imposed a substantial tax on oil products, foremost among them gasoline. This is the policy tool by which countries with net energy imports have since long held down energy consumption and forced their economies to make do with less fuel. That this can be done without loss of efficiency is evident from the experience of European countries and Japan. At the very least, the United States should have repealed the oil depletion allowance in the 1950's, to remove the direct encouragement to squander which it implied.

Nothing of the sort was done, as we know. Short-run concerns of individuals and firms were identified as the national interest, at the expense of the future, including our present. In the vital matter of energy, the American economy is as improvident as those Turkish peasants who keep too many goats and sheep, causing soil erosion to ruin their own hillside pastures and to send coarse silt into the rivers burying valuable farmlands in downstream areas in Iraq.

The simile of the Turkish peasant is instructive both for the parallel and the difference. Like the American consumer, the Turkish peasant is a captive of a system which he can not change. But unlike the American consumer, the Turkish peasant must be excused because he can not gain an overview of the system, nor could he do anything about it even if he wanted to and knew how. He is literally compelled to function within the system-in-place and to go on eroding his pastures, because he must eat tomorrow. A remote future can not concern him unless he survives long enough to see it. The Turkish government is also narrowly constrained by the conditions of a low-income, developing country. They too must provide for the next round of investments, lest the country slip back into the incurable mass poverty of a rural slum. As in most low-income countries, Turks at all levels must regard resource conservation as something which has to wait for better times.

But surely, this does not apply to the world's richest industrial nation? It should not apply to the nation but it applies to most if not all of its members, unless the nation can come together for concerted action to reform the economy, get it out of the entrenched syndrome of resource waste. With every passing year, the discounted present value of future energy supplies rises higher. The economy is already straining under the combined weight of current energy prices and current volume of energy consumption. If real costs are going to rise even higher, as seems likely at least beyond 1990, then the volume of energy use must be brought down, not just piecemeal but in a large measure.

The obstacles are many. Vested interests which would stand to lose from a salutary change are large and powerful—that follows from the size of the problem. Popular myths declare the system to be necessary just because it is in place. At every turn, one meets the argument that the automotive complex is beneficial to the economy because it is so large, when this is precisely what is wrong. Blaming the large size of the country for its level of transportation costs is also not justified since most of the car traffic is within urban areas. There are even individuals with a claim to high competence in economics who declare that intensive car traffic is essential to American dynamism. Such folklore has, of course, no support in serious analysis, and it is in curious contrast to the current scene when American auto makers have to import their new dynamism from Japan.

With such underpinnings for public opinion, and the general inertia which is analogous to the traffic congestion, politicians dare not speak out to voters on the economic changes which are necessary to get us out of the downward suction from high energy costs. When voters hear nothing much about it from their politicians, they feel justified in not asking for changes either. In this way the socio-political situation, like the housing-and-traffic system, becomes a "multiple lock-in" system, the breaking of which will necessitate a major reorientation.

A PARTISAN ISSUE?

There are weak signs of party differences in American resource policy. The shift from the forties to the fifties has a parallel in the current administration and the shift from its immediate predecessor. But these conflicts of opinion and policy concern mainly energy production, recently also environment protection. On energy consumption and the possibilities of its radical reduction through reforms of the transportation and housing systems, both parties speak in low voices.

The housing system, obviously, can only be reformed slowly, but no one even proposes the obvious start which would be in ending the tax subsidy for new home mortgages. On traffic, the solutions are simpler and could have much quicker results if the levers of traffic control (foremost of parking) were applied; but this is hardly ever mentioned. Maybe the motivations of the parties are different also on these matters, but their visible attitudes are virtually the same—they practically disregard a problem which may appear too large to tackle by the means of regular political business.

And yet, if any attempt were made to attack this problem of far reaching reform and reconstruction of the modes of operation in the American economy, party differences might be challenged to the sharpest degree yet known in this country.

Continued waste of energy, at rising costs, favors certain sectors—generally the most capital intensive and expertise intensive ones. When this development runs its course, it favors increasing income differences between higher and lower income classes. Economic reform to reduce the energy intensity of the system would, on the other hand, free resources for many of the social programs—such as health insurance—which we are now told we can not afford.

Less resource intensity and higher labor intensity in the economy would favor full employment, wider income distribution, better health protection and better quality schooling. The whole gamut of social improvement which the 1960's thought compatible with social waste, could still be affordable under a less resource wasting economic system, as evidenced by several European examples.

When the energy problem poses such a serious threat to the economic health and viability of America, it is almost academic to ask whether this is not a huge case of social waste. Some readers may still want to ask, how far can this be regarded as legitimate luxury? Does not the public enjoy its spree? The following two chapters should provide some of the answers.

Chapter 4
Curse in Disguise: The Car in America

The "freedom machine" of American folklore started out as a great liberator and ended up as heavy shackles on our economy and social system. The technical matter of how to get from here to there is compounded by addiction to speed and release from self control which are all too apparent in the automobile transportation system. As a large-scale case of social waste, it far outstrips anything that can be said of the food system. The linkages with urban over-expansion and inner-city decay, and with over-use of primary energy, are some of the direct effects of the automotive system in this country. Others are in high accident rates, in the costs of treating the effects of these, and in the strangling of other kinds of traffic and the slowing down even of auto traffic itself. Freedom has a paradox: one freedom may muscle out another one, and the balance may end up negative.

FREEDOM FROM HORSES

Contrary to what might appear to the naked eye, the automobile is only one among many features in modern technology which lead to higher gross speed in all that we are engaged in. Telegraph, telephone, radio and television, and their several applications, have in fact speeded up the transmission of information much more than anyone could ever speed up the transportation of people and goods.

Viewing it only from the perspective of the individual, the automobile made the most striking difference against all that people have had before. From the Bronze Age to the 1700's, the horse was the fastest conveyance known to man, at least outside the skiing areas of the arctic regions. In Chinese, "at once", or "right away" is expressed by a word combination which literally means "on horseback". In frontier America, the horse was so essential that horse theft often was treated as a capital crime because it could endanger the life of the human victim. Some of the expressions on early mechanical transportation are telling as to the shift in perceptions: the train locomotive was long termed "steam horse", and the automobile was hailed as a "horse-less carriage". Only gradually did the viewpoint turn around: the time came when the remaining horses in city traffic were derisively nicknamed "oat motors".

The automobile was of course far from being the first breakthrough in mechanical transportation. Starting from rail techniques in mining areas, British engineers in the early 1800's put a steam engine on wheels and ushered in a new era of cheap and increasingly rapid mass transportation of both goods and people. Some economists have tried to belittle the impact of the early railroad in America, but such attempts are based on incomplete evidence. They overlook for instance the cumulative effect of raising the rate of net savings and capital formation even fractionally, both of which must have been affected by the railroad system. They also disregard the psychological effect of breaking down age-old constraints upon human movements; characteristic is the transformation of an old hymn into a hymn-like song about the railroad ("She'll be coming 'round the mountain when she comes"). Richard Nixon in his early youth was not alone in yearning for the train as an escape to remote horizons; in rural Europe and Asia, watching the trains go by continued as a daily ritual deep into the twentieth century.

It can be argued that the railway may have made a larger difference, relatively speaking, against the stage coach than the automobile did against the horse-drawn carriage. Evidently, the railway was there first. Even today, more freight (in ton-miles) is hauled by trains than by trucks in the United States.

But the automobile meant freedom from the horse. The early railroads assumed horse drawn carriages and wagons as a supplement, to take passengers and freight from the depots along feeder roads to their final destinations. The horse-less carriage meant just that: freedom from the horse. This animal is hard to handle and is more dangerous to the unskilled than the automobile. It needs feed, water and care every day, it generates manure every day, and it needs exercise every day—horses get sick if they stand idle too long. By comparison, car ownership is far less onerous and requires less in the way of effort or exacting skills to be handled.

This may originally have meant more than the feature now most often touted: that the "freedom machine" lets you get where you want to go when you want it. The higher speed came only gradually.

As we shall see time and again, dual systems are hard to maintain. Freedom from the horse killed the draft horse, even in functions where it might have remained superior. (Milk distribution has been mentioned as a case in point because the horse, as a living being, is able to cooperate with his owner where an inanimate machine can not). The vanishing of the draft horse may have created an emotional vacuum as well. Why else would we see pseudo-romantic references to the car as if it were living and feeling, as in the television series called "My mother the Car"?

FREEDOM OF CARS

Even before there were freeways, the automobile got a free ride over the heads of the American public, the unwilling as well as the willing. As one California economist wrote many years ago, "the love affair [of the public with the car] was a shotgun wedding".

Once the automobile industry got going, it continued on its own momentum. From a few thousand cars around 1900, autos grew to many millions in the 1920's and 1930's. The Great Depression caused a slowdown in production which for a few years fell below 2 million new cars a year, down from about 4 million. Car manufacturing picked up again in the late 1930's. On the eve of World War 2, the car fleet in the United States was over 25 million passenger vehicles plus over four million trucks. The population was then just over 130 million, so the country had one car for every five persons. During the war, car production came to an almost complete standstill while trucks as well as military vehicles continued to be made in large numbers. After 1945, return to a peacetime economy meant among other things also resumption of automobile manufacturing. In recent years, well over 100 million passenger automobiles are in use, and there are some 10 million light trucks, vans and "recreational vehicles" to boost the means of individual passenger transportation. Eleven to twelve million new ones are added every year, three-fourths of them made in this country and one-fourth imported. Because of scrapping, the car fleet grows slower than that, but still it grows by a few million every year. We now have almost one car for every two persons in the population. If we count only those who may drive (excluding children, those too old or those too handicapped), the country has two cars for every three potential drivers.

The trouble with all these many cars is not so much in their number as in the ways they are used. Americans drive for all sorts of reasons, many of them frivolous or ridiculous. To hear young and healthy people complain about having to walk four blocks, one realizes that cars are used to excess. Reduced health, intoxication with speed, high rates of accidents, death and lifelong disablement, high costs of medical care are all telling on the lack of thought which gets expressed in this mass of moving wheels. Equally important, of course, is the crowding out of other, more economical means of transportation which often become unavailable even for those who need them or prefer them. The large number of automobiles also often becomes self defeating by crowded traffic slowing down the whole mass of cars. Finally, the dominant car system has caused important distortions in the economic system by absorbing large parts of the country's capital resources, as we discussed in the previous chapter.

Over-use comes from opportunity combined with the lack of reflection. Once the car has been acquired (often on credit) it appears to the user that the cost of gasoline for the next trip is cheaper than a bus ticket. This shortsighted truth is shortsighted indeed, for it disregards the car's many other costs, both direct and indirect.

In a direct sense, the car owner should consider also the share which each trip has of the general cost of car ownership: the price paid, the cost of financing (if it is on credit—otherwise the interest income foregone on the purchase price), the share in maintenance, parking costs, fines, etc. Indirectly each trip shares in costs such as street maintenance (paid from real-estate taxes) to medical costs (paid for by insurance, or Medicare-Medicaid, or by individuals emptying their savings until some go broke). Indirect costs also include the traffic police and court costs, also paid for by real-estate taxes, sometimes sales taxes or local income taxes. Finally there are the overhead disutilities of air pollution, traffic congestion and the sense of insecurity coming from careless drivers and from the use of "get-away cars" by criminals who then become more difficult to catch and to punish. How insensitive the average driver is to such overhead costs was amply demonstrated by the many ingenious stratagems by which the 55-mile speed limit (a life saver) was defeated, with increased death toll as a result. We recently got another example in the rising tide of law evasion in the case of leaded gasoline which "self-service" customers succeed in pumping into cars for which it is not intended; and the truly self-serving remarks by which many individuals defend their scoffing at the law "because so many others are doing it anyway".

Such erosion of public trust and respect for the law are among the indirect damages which the dominant car transportation system inflicts upon all of us whether we are guilty or not. The ugliness of parking places is so ever present that many people overlook them by force of habit. The loss of aesthetic feeling is also one of the corroding forces in modern society.

The automobile also means freedom from other people. An absence of human obligations is a dubious contribution to the social life of our time. Other than with neighbors and immediate work associates, the typical driver has less positive contact with other people than previously. Instead, he gets a good deal of hostile contact on the road—with other drivers as well as with those who just use their legs. Many drivers are snappy and irritable, driven by impatience and an inflated sense of power. Only seldom does this go so far as to using the car as a deadly weapon—but such cases are reported from time to time. But even without the extreme case of bodily harm, bad manners on the road are a depressing feature of the modern scene. Ironically, it took the 55-mile speed limit to unite many drivers in a camaraderie to try to defeat the law by aid of their radios.

But the hard core of the problem of a dominant passenger car transportation system is the loss of public transportation.

FREE FROM TIME TABLES, SHACKLED TO THE WHEEL

The near-death of mass transit was foreshadowed early. Except for the war years of 1942–45, rail passenger service in this country reached its peak around 1920; thereafter it declined steadily. Now it is a small remnant, all in a Federal administration struggling to keep deficits down. Bus traffic is a small part of all passenger transportation. It seems to be holding its own but amounts to little outside the few cities which because of old (pre-automobile) street layout can not offer parking areas to the extent all the newer ones do.

This takeover of car traffic from rail and bus transportation has all the earmarks of a multiple lock-in system. First the cars took over from some weak links in the railway networks and the bus systems, and marginal train and bus lines were scrapped. Then, the remaining rail and bus services lost some of their attraction because more of the trips would have to be by individual vehicles, and thus some lines which had previously been profitable became marginal and ripe for takeover. When the bus lines became thinner, more people got themselves a second car, and then the economic base for the bus system became even weaker, more of it was scrapped, until there remained only skeleton service to be maintained by public subsidy. It seldom occurs to drivers that this subsidy is part of their cost of driving. People were gradually pushed off the trains and buses whether they liked it or not. Demand for cars rose more than would have followed from freely expressed preference. Many of the new connections were indeed shotgun weddings.

Freight has held up better. Like personal transportation, rail freight also declined under the onslaught of early automotive expansion, after a peak reached around 1926—a mere half-dozen years later than in the case of personal transportation. But the decline did not become as sharp, the revival during the war was strong without being extreme, and since then rail freight has held its own. When expressed in ton-miles, more freight is now hauled by railroads in the United States than ever before—even more than during the war years. The relative share has been declining. Partly this is because pipelines are included in the total, and they are not comparable with the older modes of transportation.

Finally, even the taxi fleets have declined in many cities. An extreme case occurred in a medium-sized town with a large university. When the undergraduates were allowed to keep cars (around 1970), the taxi fleet dwindled to where it is often impossible to rely on getting a taxi within reasonable waiting time. As an additional irony, the decline of the taxi system also removed some of the jobs by which poor students tried to "work their way" through the University—there are not many such jobs in a typical "school town." The multiple lock-in here means that the opulent students took opportunities away from their struggling comrades!

The decline of railway passenger transportation in America was openly abetted by the private rail corporations. On the face of it, they wanted to simplify their operations by concentrating on cargo traffic alone. When many of them then could not even make ends meet after they had lost all passenger traffic, this points to more than low revenue in passenger traffic—the railway system has been in economic straits for other reasons, despite its indispensable role in freight traffic. Public policy was in fact favoring highway traffic, even for freight, in a degree which would not have happened if comparative costs alone had been decisive. For each ton-mile and passenger-mile, rail is cheaper in real terms than road, when all costs are honestly and completely accounted for. Convenience alone can not account for the social waste reflected in the railway crisis. Systematic favoring of road traffic, because of the higher level of consumption of fuel, hardware, and skilled manpower, has evidently also been at work.

LOSS OF OPTIONS, LOSS OF EFFICIENCY

Closing down mass transit forecloses choices, throwing large numbers of people on the highway who would rather have commuted by rail. Often this led to further increased congestion on the streets and highways which had been laid out and designed on the assumption of the previous division of labor between mass transit and individual transportation. The proverbial "long parking places" outside large cities—highways congested bumper to bumper with slow moving cars—are too well known to comment on further. The constant stopping and going in these congested situations does of course lead to very low fuel efficiency as well as loss of time and wearing down of nerves. Sitting in a taxi on the freeway between Chicago's O'Hare airport and its downtown sometimes takes two whole hours, where unhindered driving time is only twenty minutes. Ironically, this is called "rush traffic", when in fact it is snail's pace traffic. And in the Chicago Loop area, the heart of the "City Practical" (so called because it cannot be termed beautiful), car traffic around 1960 was found to proceed at about the same average speed as horse traffic had around 1900. Granted, there are more people travelling by car now than there ever were by horse power but the lack of real efficiency gain is striking and should give pause to reflect on a system that uses so many resources for so little final result.

This also means that most of what we are told about car mileage per unit of fuel spent is misleading. Engine performance is given in relation to "normal" driving conditions, not the congestion that occurs so routinely. Ironically, this also affects the comparison between cars and buses. Available studies indicate that bus traffic gets people from here to there at a cost in energy (both direct, in the buses and cars, and indirectly, in the factories and other businesses making and servicing them) which is half that of car traffic, both counted per passenger mile. But this understates the potential superiority of fuel efficiency in a bus system, because efficiency of buses is measured from actual traffic which includes many trips with few passengers and it also includes trips where "rush" traffic reduces also bus speeds to a snail's pace of stop/go, stop/go in nauseating repetition. The real efficiency comparison would of course be where the bus system were the dominant mode of transporting people, with larger loads per trip and with free use of the streets not cluttered by cars. The same is certainly true of passenger trains. They too would make much better economic sense if the system were engineered to give them the central place in the transportation system which they are both technically and economically indicated for.

The stark fact is that many people have no other means of getting there—to the job, to the stores, to wherever they have to be going. When you have no choice, it may seem as if you were acting of your own free will. It reminds us of the original Ford car: the customer could have it any color he wanted as long as he wanted it black. Now you are free to travel any way you wish as long as you wish to travel by car.

This pervasive use, often forced, of cars for commuting, shopping and even for vacations leads to a question of what kind of time these people are really having. Is driving to and from the job "free time"—or is it really a part of their work, a part of the cost of production not accounted for as such? This can not be answered merely by asserting that many people enjoy being alone by themselves behind the steering wheel of their car, because it is the only time of the day when they are allowed the complete privacy of being alone. Veteran train travellers and bus commuters know how private one can be in a crowd of strangers. This is in contrast to car pools which mean being forced into the company of neighbors who are often associates on the job—this of course is the opposite of privacy and explains why car pools tend to be unformed about as fast as they are formed. But coming back to the lone commuter or shopper: what they are doing behind the steering wheel is really a chore, a task which engages some considerable part of their personal energies and contributes substantially to their fatigue both on and off the job, including the job of shopping. This driving effort, which maximizes instead of minimizing cost in real terms, is in a very real sense a spending of a scarce resource (your personal energy), even though this never comes into the accounts of national product or income. To this extent, productivity on the job is over-rated, and cheapness of the goods purchased far away from home is also exaggerated.

By contrast, time spent in routine mass transit riding can be productive—either for rest, recreation, or learning. Commuters from Connecticut to New York City used to play cards en route. Ensconced in a train or bus seat, those who want to can read, or just plain think, or relax. Some students have been heard complaining that driving to and from a campus, when they live some distance away (e.g., on parents' farm) takes much of their day. Some could have 1–2 hours of solid reading time on the bus if the time were so used, but they can not do that behind the wheel of a car they are driving. On a train or bus, you can just doze away, if that is the best use of your time en route. But you should not do that while driving . . .

Returning to automobile driving as a luxury, which it still sometimes is, despite all: Would not pleasure driving be more pleasurable if the roads were not so cluttered by the forced over-use of the automobile? How many weekends do not start bad because they start on a congested highway at rush hour? How many vacations have not been ruined by fatigue behind the steering wheel? Thus, riches are torn to rags, and too many people know no better than to curse the other drivers, human beings as harassed as they are themselves.

The "freedom machine" thus raises some puzzling paradoxes. As always with freedom, we have to ask "free to do what?" as well as "free from what?" Freedom from the horse is no longer at issue, but the preceding discussion prompts us to suggest that the ever-present car itself means some serious loss of freedom. Under functioning mass transit, by contrast, the car's claims on our lives would be relaxed. Car-free is care-free.

Amid it all, there is also a question about freedom from danger.

HAZARDOUS TO YOUR LIFE AND HEALTH

Depending on what page of the statistics you look at, there are either 18 million or 25 million traffic accidents per year in the United States, and nearly all of them involve private cars. Fifty thousand American lives are lost each year in the highway carnage, not far behind the number lost in Viet Nam in ten years of warfare. Millions are injured every year, but the statistics do not appear to tell how many become crippled for life, or what it would cost to restore all those whom only a millionaire's budget could afford to restore to full health and mobility.

Since 1920, about two and a half million Americans have lost their lives in traffic accidents, again nearly all in road traffic, with the passenger automobile as the main culprit. Traffic deaths of railway passengers and railway employees are a minute fraction of the death toll of the highways, even in the heyday of rail passenger service, a time when technology was less developed than now and over-all security (technically available) was less than can be obtained now under full maintenance of equipment.

We do get some data on costs of accidents. Such as they are, they indicate that it now costs the national economy over 50 billion dollars per year to pay for car accidents. That is not part of the car costs as conventionally measured, but it would increase those conventional costs by one-fourth if it were. The costs reported include medical treatment—the treatment received, not that which would be required if money had been no object. The costs also include loss of work time and a few other items such as funeral costs.

But this is not the whole story about cars and health. Air pollution can kill those with an ailing heart. It even hurts joggers and runners who inhale too much carbon monoxide. Lack of exercise in the routinely car-borne population leads to flabby muscles, to be built up only at the cost of gymnasium workouts or other more or less expensive, special arrangements. The healthy habit of walking between home and transit stops gives you as much without paying a cent for it, just a bit of wear on shoesoles. And, we have been told since some time, the number one health complaint of adult Americans is backache. And the number one cause of backache is . . . the automobile! How much all of this detracts from life as it might be in a less car bound existence can only be vaguely guessed, for lack of precise information.

Related to this is the intoxication with speed, which probably contributes as much to accidents as does the widespread habit of driving while under the influence of alcohol and other intoxicants. Speed is in itself a drug which changes our perceptions, and to many it also enlarges the ego—as if the engine were an expression of personal ability in the driver rather than of technical competence of the car making industry.

The value of high speed is generally over-rated in modern society. Other than in accident risks, speed with vehicles has the indirect disadvantage that the speeder feels relieved of the need for pensiveness in making decisions. The matter has some analogy with speed in communications and financial transactions which also can go to excess. Electronic banking is certainly a very mixed blessing, not only because of the increased risk of theft but also by the greater invitation to impulse action, which is so evident in today's credit system. Less reliance on invariably speedy transportation might lead to more considering of the question, is this trip necessary—or even desirable?

FINDING A WAY OUT OF THE MAZE

As with energy in general, any attempt at debating the traffic system in America runs into heavy resistance on emotional grounds. This in itself is a bad symptom of what the car system has done to our society. When it can not even be discussed rationally, it must have displaced other, more essential human concerns. "We are married to our cars" is the obscene answer I sometimes get from college students in their twenties. An official in the Carter Administration's Department of Energy once related to me how he and some colleagues had been near mobbed by a hardhat audience in a northeastern industrial city; these workers would not hear of any limitations to their use of gasoline. "It would be political suicide to tell the truth about energy" is a phrase I have heard from politicians in very different parts of the political spectrum. The riots and shooting among truck drivers on the highways which accompanied the first oil embargo (1973) was repeated recently to protest the enactment of a very modest increase in the gasoline tax—a measure which was long overdue and would make itself felt only gradually. Such episodes exemplify the low level of rationality Americans often show when faced with the need to reform their habits in squandering fuel. This emotional resistance is the greatest in regard to cars and trucks. Here it often sounds as if "gas at the pump" were among our constitutional rights.

For the over-use of cars for commuting and shopping, the technical solution is simplicity itself. It is based on the fact that you can not drive for commuting or shopping without having access to parking space. Whoever controls parking, controls traffic. A parked car is a sitting duck for controls. This is intuitively evident, and there are some telling examples from the application of controls against on-street parking. Details will be discussed in the last chapter. If this lever is intelligently applied, mass transit could in a few years be back in the position of principal mode of conveyance for persons, with immense savings of fuel, materials, industrial capacity, health and life, and the quality and dignity of life. Why nothing of the sort is tried is explained in part by the comments made above about politics. Other parts of the explanation will come from examining the urban system in the United States, itself the scene of social waste on a gigantic scale.

Chapter 5
From Community to Traffic Machine: Disintegration of the American City

The old-world city is a place in which to live and work, with transportation arranged to serve these purposes. The American city once was something similar, but since the automobile took over transportation, it also took over the city. Most American cities can now be described as traffic machines in which living and working are made to accommodate the dominant force of automotive transportation.

This inversion of roles has enormous economic effects, many of them negative. The larger the role of transportation, the less efficient is the city as a home for people. High transportation overhead costs lead to high real-estate overheads: a high rate of conversion of land from rural to urban use, high levels of costs for streets, lights, sanitary sewers etc. Vast expanses of housing and rapid transportation between them, and between them and the commercial areas, areas of employment etc., make it easy to maintain segregation in housing, rendering worse existing ethnic and sociocultural cleavages in American society. Specifically, it consolidates the existence of areas and groups of people for whom drug use is commonplace, and for whom therefore organized crime is a service organization. The continuous spilling out of the city toward its periphery joins forces with tax advantages to drain inner-city areas of their economic substance, causing accelerated attrition of physical assets and chronic submerging of human assets. Along with the ghettos and slums, the bypassed older city areas often become "throw-away cities", discarded by the developers of new areas with about as little thought as aluminum cans and plastic bottles are thrown to the wayside.

AMERICA THE RURAL

The nineteenth-century image of the United States as a country of farms and rural small towns was changing already by the turn of the century. However, it was only around 1920 that the urban and rural populations came into near balance. This was just about the same time when the automobile was poised to come along in large numbers. It was also the time when railroad passenger traffic reached its peacetime peak. In a sense, however, the rural environment may still have prevailed at that time. A substantial part of the urban population was then in rural small towns, many of which have since then disappeared. The population of the places that are now cities had not yet reached the halfway mark of the total population of the country.

In 1920, the population of the United States was about 106 million, or less than half of what it is now. Since then, urban areas have taken up nearly all of the population increase. Urban population is thus now more than three times as large as in 1920, while rural population has lingered on at about the same level since then. Recent statistics indicate some resurgence of rural population, but this, like the near-stability of rural population since 1920, is an illusion caused by the way the statistics are organized. In reality, most of what now passes for rural people are in fact urban people living in the ever more nebulous outer fringes of the cities, at some distance from urban corporate limits. Disappearance of many older small towns—some to the point of being plowed under—only accentuates how complete the changeover has been. The many "ex-urban" settlement areas of urban character belong effectively to the urban system as it now functions and are tied to urban centers (and urban periphery-areas such as shopping centers) in much the same ways as do the officially recognized suburban areas. Favored by lighter tax burdens and not much hampered by slightly longer distances, these "ex-urban" settled areas represent the ultimate consequence of the disintegration of the original city.

OLD CITIES AND NEW

There are of course cities which were laid out so early that their inner parts could not be taken over by the automobile as completely as the newer ones, or the more recently enlarged ones. New York City, in the extreme case, is too compactly built in its older parts to have parking places for all who work there, and so has to continue relying on mass transit. High costs of parking is epitomized by parking areas on the top of medium-high skyscrapers. Something similar goes for Boston, Philadelphia and New Orleans, all of which have continued to have strong city centers. Such cities continue also to have "profile" or "personality", reflecting more or less distinctive cultural characteristics which make them continuing and indispensable assets in the life of the nation.

Some others were not so lucky. Extreme is the case of Washington, D.C., which was laid out, at the advice of a French city planner (Lenfant) to meet the needs of mob control by artillery as experienced in revolutionary France. Thus Washington got its grand avenues, with their complex triple orientation, while the city area was still, for the most part, cow pastures surrounding the planned new streets. Gradually, as the former green spaces were filled with concrete, the result became a peculiar variety of the traffic-machine concept of a city. As such, it has too little human attraction to be a permanent home except for janitors and their unemployed relatives.

The newer cities had none of these constraints, either from old-world layout or from military-planning experimentation. Typically, a place such as Los Angeles grew without much planning, just as real-estate developers might find it convenient to make money. Instead of a community, Los Angeles is a loose clustering of built-up areas having little in common except the network of streets, including some urban freeways. An even more extreme case is Houston, Texas, where a population (in the city and its suburbs) of two million occupy built-up areas equalling those of New York and Chicago combined. These expanses of settled areas, and intervening wasteland, are so vast that not only can they not be served by practically functioning mass transit, but in some areas they can not even support decent sewer systems. The driving force was "real-estate development" which is shorthand for profits made in over building the outer fringes of the cities. Here this system has outdone itself worse than anywhere else.

What the big cities do in a big way, the smaller ones emulate on a scale that touches upon the ridiculous. Communities of less than 100,000 inhabitants—a mere fraction of what the older metropolises had in their heydays—find too little parking space near where their old centers are and so build peripheral shopping malls, some with extremely lavish parking areas to surround them. Such "market places" not only drain the old city center of commercial activity. They also attract customers from rural small towns to the point where those rural places can not keep up their marketing systems any more. Rapid succession of ever newer peripheral shopping malls renders some of the older ones—older by a decade or two—obsolete before they are physically worn out. Occasionally a new peripheral shopping mall turns out to be such a mistake that it is closed after a year or two. Such continuing over expansion at the periphery causes a continuing chain of social waste in the use of space, buildings, overhead investments, etc. Overlapping authority for zoning between town and rural county sometimes causes an unhealthy competition leading municipalities to accommodate more commercial development than there is any use for. When the old city center dies, by instalments, more or less perfunctory attempts are made to revive it, only to cause more money to be sunk into hopeless cases. At best, a county-seat town may gain some reconsolidation of its center around the activities of the courthouse, the jail, and a convention hotel. Often its limited space is then encumbered with parking structures to increase the areas where cars may be left while the owners use the ever more scattered facilities of the anemic city center.

H.U.D. AND THE HIGHWAY SYSTEM

The need for a Federal Department of Housing and Urban Development resulted very directly from the ways in which car transportation was allowed to take over the cities. The urban system has just kept on flowing outward, regardless of the consequent asset destruction of the inner cities. Much of our urban problems come from over investment in space intensive housing and commercial development. The Chicago metropolitan area in Illinois (not counting the suburbs in Indiana), for instance, expanded its built-up area by 45 percent in 11 years (1964–75), even with very little population increase. Older cities, such as New York, have also suffered a great deal from the combined effects of excessive suburban expansion (in part into Connecticut, in this case). Blighted areas going to outright ruin, such as the South

Bronx, are the victims of thoughtless expansion elsewhere combined with inadequate tax systems.

In some extreme cases, the automobile system assaulted the cities by the new concept of the urban freeway—a major street with limited access from other streets and having its main function in providing long-distance connections with the rural and inter-city Federal highway systems. This was an extension, into the cities, of a concept originally designed for rural areas and for transportation connecting cities with each other.

When the interstate system of Federal highways was first started, in the 1950's, much was made of the need to provide transportation for military forces, in similar ways as Germany had provided for its armies to move between the eastern and western war fronts. As a strategy concept for the United States, the analogy with Germany was of course specious to begin with. No one was envisaging a two-front war with Mexico and Canada. Ironically, modern military equipment (such as inter-continental rockets) is often too large and heavy to be served by the interstate highway system; the intersections are really built for civilian traffic and some would have to be blown up to accommodate heavy military traffic. So much the less reason do we have for accepting even the original rationale of the interstate highway system at face value.

It can in fact be argued strongly that the builders of the Federal interstate highway system went to excess even in the rural areas. Some of the means sunk into Federal superhighways might have been used more rationally by strengthening the railway systems, especially the physical upkeep of the rail beds. Less emphasis on highways would of course also have made the railways retain more of the traffic which now went to trucks and cars. This question of superhighways in rural areas is one of degree: some of them were no doubt justified even if not all of them were.

But the metropolitan freeway is now widely recognized as a colossal policy mistake. There was not the shadow of a military rationale here: if anything, military transports must bypass the cities, not run through them. Instead of helping transportation within the cities, the metropolitan freeways have severed parts of a city from each other and favored transportation beween suburbs across the city, thus accelerating the draining of the inner city more effectively than anything else could have done. How distorting this can be has only slowly come to attention. For instance, when Watts, Los Angeles, exploded in riots, burning and looting in 1965, most immediate comments only blamed bad race relations. Two years later, an alert reporter pointed to the Los Angeles Freeway as a source of severe economic deprivation to the Watts area which was "bottled up" by the freeway, cut off by its no-access ribbon of concrete from much of the rest of the city. Decline of bus transportation pulled in the same direction: the Watts people got less access to both the job opportunities and shopping areas in most of Los Angeles. With lower incomes made worse because of increased unemployment, the Watts people had even less possibility of moving about when many of them were not even able to afford cars. Because they then had to rely more exclusively than before on local merchants in the area, the Watts people also became easier victims of exploitation by such merchants. The looting was not entirely senseless: some of it was revenge.

Only after the urban freeways had done a great deal of damage to the cities where they have been built, did it become possible by much political struggle to put a stop to further, even more senseless projects of this kind. Thus, for instance, an urban freeway had been planned for New Orleans in a way that would have ruined the old city center, the French-Spanish "vieux carré". The road building engineers were thinking exclusively in terms of what they term "vehicular benefits", as if those could exist in a vacuum. The long fought-about plan for a crosstown expressway in Chicago now also appears to have been laid to rest. If it had been built, it would have destroyed the city it was supposed to serve—by pumping traffic across the metropolitan area it would just have served the suburbs at both ends. But in Washington, D.C., the much needed Metro (underground railway) was long held hostage to the completion of the urban freeway system. The highway and automobile interests wanted to make sure that the Metro would not be allowed to make economic sense in competition with surface traffic favorably treated no matter how congested.

With such underpinnings of destructive forces, much of what passes for "urban renewal" is foreordained to failure—throwing good money after the bad. The central city can live only if it is given deliberately the role of first-rate center. It can not linger on as a poor relation of the corn-field shopping mall.

CITY LAYOUT AND ENERGY WASTE

The National Energy Plan issued in April, 1977 under the Carter administration, stated among other things (in its preface) that part of the energy problem in this country is that, as a result of cheap energy in the past, the United States developed "a stock of capital goods—such as homes, cars, and factory equipment—that uses energy inefficiently".

The statement can be broadened to include the way our cities are set up—the wider physical framework for buildings and traffic. Transportation and housing, as we now know, consume most of the energy in this country, so it is no surprise to find that we here have a large part of all the energy waste. The "traffic machine" concept of the city is also among the most difficult parts of the problem to turn around, as we shall see on the examples of parking areas and shopping systems. Past mistakes have been "cast in concrete", and the trends that made them have not been stopped. The drift toward less and less energy efficient city layout continues even now, since hoped-for economic expansion to a large extent is supposed to take the form of new single-family dwellings as well as new cars. Over-use of automobiles for routine purposes is also discouraged, if at all, in half-hearted ways only. Continuing government attitudes since many years, the current prevailing scheme for economic recovery still relies on the automotive complex as a "growth sector". The traffic system, of course, needs no positive encouragement any more to go on as before. Much of it has become a "multiple lock-in" system where the parts of the system determine each other in ways which individuals and firms are unable to break by their own force, even when they might want to do so. Even cities are at a loss handling such problems all by themselves. The city which refuses to arrange suitable re-zoning of land to accommodate a new peripheral shopping mall, for instance, will just lose this commercial opportunity to some other, more accommodating city.

City layout also has other consequences for energy systems. For instance, one of the large causes of low energy efficiency in this country is the failure to exploit steam co-generation from fuel-fired electric generation plants: the system whereby the plant delivers steam for space heating along with the electricity going to the power grid. Such a system is more efficient in using fuel—the total of the steam and the electricity delivers more effect than can be obtained from generating steam and electricity in separate establishments. Such a system also means staying with plants of moderate size, because if they are very large, the ductworks by which steam is transported to where it is to be used would stretch over too vast distances. This also rules out serving vast expanses of detached family dwellings on large lots by co-generated steam. But even in the central parts of a city this system would require a management attitude different from that of most utility companies. As localized monopolies they tend to prefer large sized plants. The extreme case is the nuclear power plant which for some time was high in the favor of utility executives, until their high cost became evident. Nuclear plants have to be very large—much too large for steam co-generation systems, and they should be located some distance from urban centers.

The least inefficient way to heat urban buildings would likely be by a combination of electric heat pumps in some blocks or neighborhoods, and steam from co-generating plants in some others. Total effect of the fuel burned would be higher than in any other way of using primary fuel. But that would require two things: power plants of modest size, and planned, relatively compact layout of city areas to be served by such plants, with no intervening wasteland and a minimum of areas which are not participating in the heating system, such as parking areas. Such plants would of course also have to be equipped with highly efficient scrubbing systems to avoid pollution. There are some such systems already in operation, but they show no tendency to become "mainstream" in the mass of urban areas which are already built.

It is generally agreed that past years of cheap energy have put in place huge amounts of buildings which use energy inefficiently because of the ways in which they are built. Better insulation designs are now available but it is by no means clear that they are being widely used. It appears, to the contrary, that the people for whom new homes are being built largely prefer to economize on such features, because, like the drivers exceeding the 55-mile speed limit, they are concerned about immediate advantages such as limiting the acquisition price of the house and the way they are going to finance it—they try to avoid large capital charges. For future energy efficiency, the initial capital expenditures ought to be larger than in the past, but this is particularly difficult to drive home at a time when the cost of capital—the interest rate—is held artificially high by current economic policy.

One negative standard is particularly destructive: many large city buildings such as multi-story office structures in central city areas are equipped not only with single-sheet glass windows which lose heat to the atmosphere at a high rate, but they also often have windows which can not be opened. The latter feature is in the interest of using air conditioning with more efficiency, including the keeping out of the street smog which comes from the many cars out there. Ventilation then has to be by air conditioning all round the year, no matter how dubious such a system is for health reasons. There may be several explanations for such a tendency in construction. One is in "technological over-kill", the tendency of some engineers to use a technology just because it is available. Another is of course in the smog problem which will be solved only when city traffic becomes a good deal different from what it is now.

COMMUTER TRAFFIC

Daily job commuting is easily one of the least productive uses of energy and of urban space in this country. Sixty million Americans proceed from home to place of work, and back again, by fifty million cars (and trucks), for an average occupancy ratio of 1.2 persons per vehicle. Much of this traffic takes place in the morning and afternoon rush hours, and some of it in the before-and-after lunch rushes. Fuel efficiency, measured in miles-per-gallon (mpg) is just about the worst conceivable. When commuters are out in force, all cars become "gas guzzlers". By being numerous, commuter cars waste fuel and time for each other as well as for the buses and other traffic.

Several studies have been made to show that very large energy savings can be obtained if commuting is by mass transit, to say nothing of cycling and walking. But the studies agree to say that a large-scale transition is unlikely to come about by itself. Past policy has shied away from interfering with the physical framework for traffic. Market forces were assumed to reflect the relevant economic realities—this is what was assumed, for instance, in the Statement of National Transportation Policy issued by Secretary Coleman in the Ford Administration in September 1975.

Discussion of market forces belongs in several places in this book, and this is one of them because the "cast-in-concrete" physical framework of city traffic is one of the most powerful market modifiers one can find. Speaking in general terms, market forces are nothing but the expression of the economic interests which happen to be in power for the time being. With different income distribution and different public policies—say, in the 1950's when the critical decisions affecting transportation were made—we would now have different market forces, also for transportation. What we now know about future higher energy costs (especially capital costs) makes it necessary that we depart from the market relations of the day and use traffic controls which will anticipate long-term conditions to come. Between very high energy prices and administrative controls, the former have the disadvantage that they will bear down most on those who can least afford them without for that sake necessarily making a reduced level of energy use more efficient. Fuel prices and/or rationing may also cut down most on recreation travels—a legitimate luxury—but leave the commuting system unchanged or nearly so.

Feasibility of commuting without cars can be studied in areas where such systems are already in place, mainly for historical reasons, such as some older cities in the United States. Some public agencies, such as NASA and the Pentagon, also have far fewer parking spaces than employees, and thus implicitly enforce commuting by means other than individual driving.

SHOPPING TRAFFIC AND CAR-FREE ZONES

Transportation systems for shopping are as obviously overloaded as are those for commuting. Downtown areas increasingly suffer from shortage of parking space, and there is really no way out of it as long as shopping relies on intensive use of individual cars. Each time a downtown area acquires more parking space, it also creates greater distances between parts of the shopping district itself. It is routine for a good-size shopping center to be surrounded by five to ten acres of parking spaces, and even larger areas are not uncommon. Parking structures are somewhat less space-demanding but in exchange they represent large investments which only at high cost can be converted to other uses. The net result of the parking dilemma in downtown areas is that large parts of the stores are moved to the periphery, causing over supply of selling places and still more use of land for parking. A recently built "regional shopping center" just outside a middle-sized town in Illinois took up 80 acres of prime farmland, most of it for parking, leaving behind vacant buildings in the "throw-away city" of the old center in town. Like the American farmers, supermarkets are efficient in what they are doing, but their services fit into a larger system which is inefficient by the social waste it leads to—in the use of fuel, land, and infrastructure investment in over-large urban areas.

Car-free zones in downtown areas, and shopping systems not depending on individual cars for transportation of customers and goods, are now widespread in European cities. In general they are also very successful from a commercial point of view. Beginning with off-street galleries as in Paris and The Hague, there are substantial areas without any but purely local access by automobiles, for instance in Stockholm, Cologne and Rome. In the United States we have less experience with this, but there is some of it. A number of cities have been experimenting in this direction in recent years. The time should be ripe for drawing together the experience and showing what can be accomplished.

PARKING AREAS AND ALTERNATIVE LAND USE

Among the disadvantages of intensive car traffic in urban areas is the amount of land now used for parking. This is especially striking in the case of commuter cars. Every car has to have a permanent home where it is at night. Commuter cars have two, for most of the commuter spaces are empty at night. Ground level parking occupies land at a rate of about 150 cars to the acre, including the space needed to get in and out of the parking area. With 50 million commuter vehicles, most of them parked near the place of work, commuter parking occupies about one-third of a million acres in this country. Most of this land is in places where it gets in the way of other activity. With five commuter cars for every 22-23 persons of the population, a middle sized city of 100,000 people easily gets commuter parking space of about 150 acres, or something like one percent of total city area. Much of this is in business districts, industrial parks, university campuses and other economically intensive areas where the parking spaces are a considerable fraction of the land area. Thus, parking areas cause substantial delays in movement between buildings. They also necessitate longer distances for power lines, sewers, heat ducts, and so on. Most of these areas are also areas where the real-estate value per square foot of land is high, a fact seldom mentioned in connection with the cost of accommodating employee parking— usually, only the current costs of maintenance are mentioned then, while real-estate costs are treated as fixed overheads.

The parallel diseconomy in shopping areas was discussed above. Parking areas are used by several different vehicles during the day, but even so they may take up as much space as the commuter areas, because those for shopping are geared to meet peak-hour demand. In both cases, transportation actually feeds on itself by creating some of the distances that must be overcome by transportation.

In all urban areas, and especially those of intensive economic use, land is at a premium and parking areas could be put to more productive uses. Using them as building sites would give the city's central parts a more compact layout and reduce overhead costs. Use as recreation areas, such as tennis courts and green space, would enhance the aesthetic appeal and the healthiness of the city. Eventually some of this space may be used to build solar collectors, for local heating or for auxiliary electric generation.

Basically our cities have the instruments they need to control wasteful land layout in and around themselves. In practice, not much use is made of these instruments. Competition between firms is compounded by competition with nearby communities. The desire to attract new economic activity leads the cities to a level of hospitality toward business which takes precedence over all forms of land-saving. Without over-arching rules of conduct to tell communities what they should and should not do, it will not be possible to arrest sprawl and peripheral urban development with the consequent formation of urban-fringe wasteland. The location of a new industrial plant or merchandise outlet may appear very important for the community which gets it or fails to get it, but in the aggregate of the national economy it makes very little difference in most cases. The lavish use of land in the cities and associated overhead costs do in any event cause diseconomies which should be of concern to both the national and the local economy.

BLIGHTED AREAS, BLIGHTED PEOPLE

The general relaxing of distance constraints through more rapid transportation has also led to less contact between people of different backgrounds and so contributed to sharpening the tendency in America for people to live in neighborhoods which are homogenous both in income level, in ethnic traditions, and in subculture. In the Old World, it was among the positive traits of the central city as a community that members of many social classes could live in the same apartment building—on different floors, for sure, but they met in stairways and elevators, and they shared the same *concierge*. In programmatically classless America, the real classes of society are kept more strictly apart, courtesy the automobile system. The glamor ghettos of the rich and the well-to-do crown their achievements by well-equipped "neighborhood schools" which they want to protect against integration by busing so that there will be no undesirable contacts with the children of the disadvantaged ghettos. The latter, of course, become negative poles from which all flee who have the means to live elsewhere. The example of Watts, Los Angeles, is one among many where deprivation became cumulative because it was concentrated. Concentration is enforced by the automobile, the highway system, and the gradual decline in mass transit. The automobile may seem like a freedom machine to the well-to-do because they never reflect on its indirect disadvantages. At the lower end of the income scale, those who can not afford automobiles are so much the more constrained in their movements when there is almost no other way to move about.

How neglected city centers can be was illustrated in a curious way a number of years ago when it was revealed that the Census of Population had missed several million Americans. In a country with such advanced statistical and computer services, this was a remarkable feat indeed. These "lost people" (lost to the Census, that is) were not evenly spread across American society. Instead, they were concentrated mainly in certain inner-city areas into which some Census agents did not go because they were scared.

Such neglect in the enumeration of people did more than violate the original purpose of the Census which is (ever since 1790) to help apportion political representation—in the U.S. House of Representatives, in State legislatures, and other representative bodies. The forgotten people, unless re-captured by subsequent surveys, would be under-represented politically.

Forgetting some of the city slums would of course also lead to underestimating their size and the extent of their problems.

The spread of concentrated poverty areas is not overtly planned by elected governments either Federal, State, or local. Instead it is planned and enforced by unelected governments in banks, insurance firms and real-estate enterprises. By "red-lining" of areas which they designate as not credit worthy or not insurable, bankers and insurers issue self-fulfilling prophecies of continued decay even of properties which were perfectly sound to begin with. Without credit for purchase and for upkeep, and without insurance, such areas are foredoomed to the decay which red-lining says is already there. Once this mechanism has been set in motion, there is no way, under the present dispensation, of stopping the downward suction. No one with the financial means to keep up or to upgrade a decayed but structurally sound building would do so in a neighborhood against which the odds have been deliberately stacked in this way.

There are a few exceptions. Here and there, determined people form "neighborhood associations" to stop or reverse residential decay. Official policy also tries to upgrade some neglected urban areas by designating them as "development areas". None of this is likely to amount to very much, from coast to coast, as long as the "market forces" of red-lining, speculation in slum housing, and over-building of the urban fringes are given a free hand to do business as usual. Reform action against such forces is, as with urban renewal in most cases, throwing good money after the bad.

The decay of older city areas is prompted and accelerated by short-term profit motives centering around real-estate developments tending to over-extend the city. The decay was started, to a large extent, by the ease of transfer by automobile, combined with inadequate tax laws. The disintegration of the cities leads consistently to loss of physical assets in decaying buildings and in infrastructure poorly kept up in the center while expansion at the periphery continues as mindlessly as ever.

The destruction of physical assets is paralleled by the waste of humanity among those who have to linger on in the decaying areas. The poverty ghetto is compounded by its tie-ins with the subcultures of drug use and organized crime. The result is further compounded by low quality schools in poverty areas, and by discrimination by "race", which is mainly a cover term for subculture. How all of this leads to waste of human assets, will be discussed in the following three chapters.

Chapter 6
From Prohibition to Drug War

The persistent tendency in America to legislate selectively against some sins, such as addiction to drugs, while condoning some others, such as addiction to high-speed traffic, poses a continuing riddle. When will the lessons be learned about the futility and the backfiring of moral repression in a free society? If intelligence is defined as the ability to learn from experience, then American public policy appears remarkably lacking in intelligence wherever practical issues are loaded with blind emotions. The drug enforcement syndrome continues to produce one of the most unmitigated cases of social waste ever seen.

How emotional, as opposite to rational, the debate really is, becomes evident when we note that the tendency to restrict drugs is the strongest among people who call themselves "conservatives", which means they are opposed to several other possible restrictions on our lives such as gun control, industrial responsibility for pollution and chemical dumps, and the use of taxes to support the health of fellow citizens.

PROHIBITION AND SYNDICATE CRIME

The "noble experiment" of outlawing alcoholic beverages in the United States went on for fourteen years. The Eighteenth Amendment to the U.S. Constitution was proposed in 1917 and went into effect in January 1920, a year after it had been enacted. It was repealed by the Twenty-First Amendment, which took effect in December, 1933.

No one denies that Prohibition was a colossal failure. Whatever it may have done to the drinking habits of programmatically law-abiding people, it contributed little to the alcohol problem as such. Worse, by ineffectual enforcement it helped finance organized crime which thereby was made more intractable than ever before. By rendering prohibited booze harder to get, the law handed more lucrative business to criminal organizations who thus got more economic muscle by which to frustrate law enforcement. This result of Prohibition did not disappear with Repeal. Instead it became the base from which organized criminals could expand into still other activities, among them the drug trade. The Godfather's New York and Al Capone's Chicago are somber legacies with which American society appears to have some difficulty coming to terms. Witness all the semi-romantic hoopla around a cosmetic image of the "Godfather" as if he had been an almost moral figure instead of an unconscionable parasite on society.

Leaving aside for the moment the human consequences, we may analyze the drug prohibition syndrome as an exhibit of some rather elementary economic principles. If these principles had been clearly understood, they should have ruled out the police state approach to such problems. The parallel with Prohibition is complete, for alcohol too is a drug. To this day, alcoholism is a larger problem than all other drugs combined.

These economic principles include: first, demand creates supply; second, a successful supply base creates more demand; and third, repression creates the analogy of scarcity, which is the best possible precondition for commercial and financial success, whether in legitimate business or in syndicate crime organization.

DEMAND CREATES SUPPLY

Prohibition of alcohol did not eliminate the demand for alcoholic beverages, and neither has outlawing of other drugs done away with the demand for them. This demand was there to begin with and was the ostensible reason for laws prohibiting what are euphemistically termed "controlled substances"—euphemistically, for in reality these substances are entirely out of control.

In the absence of an ironclad police state, which no one was prepared to propose and which hardly could have been made to function in America, the continued demand for booze elicited its own supply. Absence of legitimate supply sources raised the profit levels of the illegal sources and made sure that effective demand would be met, at prices which represented—as in elementary economic analysis—the equilibrium between supply costs and the prices which consumers were willing and able to pay under the circumstances. Supply costs, of course, included the incidence of police success, such as it was.

In a country as opposed to government edict as the United States, the act of defying the system became one more motive to buy the prohibited goods, over and above the original motive which is to escape from life's pressures into intoxication. The fact that rich people had been able to stock their cellars while the wares were still legal, and thus could go on drinking legally (only the manufacture and sale of alcohol had been outlawed) also added social prestige to continuing alcohol habits. In its wake, Prohibition left behind the unhealthy American habit of concentrating one's alcohol intake to the "cocktail hour" before a meal, instead of using the drinks as a spice with the food in which case the drug damage is less.

The feeling among many people that the prohibited pleasure is in fact their legitimate due has also played a role, both under Prohibition and later in the trade with heroin and other drugs. Outlawing what many people do not regard as criminal contributes to weakening the respect for the law. The Mafia, for all its destructiveness, is thus in many areas looked upon as a kind of service outfit toward which customers feel a degree of implied loyalty: it delivers, for instance, the heroin, and it extends a degree of protection to its loyal collaborators. The police easily becomes an alien or even an enemy in drug-infested urban slums.

In the case of heroin (and some other drugs) there comes in a second destructive effect of repression which may not have been as important with alcohol: the "supply-side" economics of recruiting new addicts, for market expansion.

SUPPLY CREATES DEMAND

The principle is well known from legitimate business, especially in luxury goods: sellers—above all of goods which are new on the market or not in general use—try to reach out toward customers not previously exposed to their wares. In the case of the heroin trade, the principle has worked with a vengeance, defeating many times over the ostensible purpose of repression.

In its simplest form, it is this. Because heroin is prohibited, the retail price is high. Without repression, it would be much cheaper;

Chinese coolies, abjectly poor though they were, usually were able to afford their opium. Because the drug is expensive under repression, there is high profit in the trade and even more so in expanding the market. And because, consequently, the habit is expensive, many users help finance their habit by recruiting new users—new addicts from among people who might never have been hooked on heroin had they not been led into the habit by "street pushers". Other addicts, of course, finance their habit by street crime such as mugging and purse snatching, more or less protected in doing so by the same syndicate which gets the proceeds of their robberies by way of the heroin price. The main point is that old established customers become marketing agents, actively promoting the merchandise. The process is not much different from other merchandise which uses local door-to-door sales agents. The difference is that repression itself by causing the price to be high, thereby increases the rate of profit in the trade and accelerates the recruiting of new addicts.

The backfiring could not have been more complete. The point to rub in, until we never forget it, is that drug repression actually makes the drug problem worse instead of bringing a cure for it. Apart from the active recruiting of new addicts, repression also makes the problem worse by its price effect and the resulting high rate of profit for the captains of organized crime.

SCARCITY IS GOOD FOR BUSINESS

Yet another piece of simple economic analysis will show how repression becomes automatically self defeating. Limited as are the successes of drug law enforcement, these "successes" always backfire for a very simple reason. When the police succeed in seizing some drug supplies and arrest some culprits, they momentarily reduce the supply on the street market. Then the street price goes up. The merchandise not seized by the police becomes more valuable, it fetches higher prices. Higher incomes then go to the drug dealers who were not arrested. With larger financial resources, the surviving drug dealers can organize their trade even more efficiently; they find even more ingenious ways of evading the police. Any inroad which the police may have made into the drug market is thus quickly neutralized. The amount of drugs on the market is at length undiminished or even increased. Only the cost has gone up—both the cost of the market supply to the addicts (and indirectly to all of us, through the damage to society) and the cost of policing which is also paid for by all of us, ineffectual though it is.

This case of artificial scarcity favoring the business concerned is fully in line with other forms of social waste as explained in general terms in the first chapter of this book and as illustrated in other chapters. In a sense, the attempts at policing is just what the surviving drug dealers would want. They have no objection to some of their competitors being thrown in prison, just as farmers have no objection to crop failures on someone else's fields. The analogy with legitimate business only strengthens the conviction of the drug dealers—and many of their customers too—that they are in fact business men performing a service demanded by market forces.

RICH CROOKS, POOR POLICE

The wages of sin are many times larger than anything society is willing to spend on the curbing of sin, by controlling of "controlled substances". Even to try would be self-defeating, for yet another economic reason: a police force many times larger than at present could not be paid enough to maintain quality.

As an examle, let us take a campaign flourish once uttered by a "law-and-order" Presidential candidate. The fact that he was a nuisance candidate, not a serious one, is not important; he was capable of affecting the outcome by splitting the vote. To combat crime in the Nation's capital (then the crime capital of the country), this candidate vowed to put "a policeman every ten yards" along Washington's streets. To do something like that, he would of course have had to recruit many times more policemen than were already on the payroll. This would have meant reaching deep into the labor force, of the city and of the country (assuming that this was not going to be an exclusive window dressing for Washington). Then one of two things would have had to happen. Either this candidate would have had to hire as police large numbers of honest and efficient individuals from other walks of life. This would among other things also have caused shortages of skilled manpower across the whole economy. To attract and to retain all these capable people as police officers, the wage bill would have become crushing, it would in fact far exceed all the damage which crime does to society. Or else the police force would have to be expanded by including large numbers of individuals which were not doing much of any value elsewhere in the economy. Paying them what they were worth would not cost so much, but such a police force could not be kept honest, many of them would soon be "on the take".

The quantity problem of law enforcement has been shown many times. One instance is the recent crackdown in Florida which was made somewhat successful by concentrating unusually large police forces in that one area, because the drug trade seemed to be particularly intensive there. The result was that most of the trade simply moved to other areas in the country. The problem then came up, could all our coasts and borders be policed as intensively as was the case in the Florida crackdown? The answer, once again, is negative. A real police success, across the whole country, is too expensive, especially in a society as riddled with all forms of social waste as the United States.

The quantity problem of controlling drug trade is compounded, under the present legal rules, by the size of the auxiliary army which the Mafia can muster in its war against law and order. Their agents include not only the street pushers; at least passively, the auxiliary army also includes most of the addicts. Because the addicts are technically criminal, they tend to side with the drug dealers more willingly than they would if they were not in legal jeopardy of becoming prison inmates. Witnesses for the prosecution are often hard to find, and it is made harder when so many of the potential witnesses are themselves members of the system being prosecuted.

The business aspect of the drug trade leads to a curiously paradoxical conclusion: since the police raise the profits of the drug trade, and since the continued success of the drug trade leads to a clamoring for more police (including better police salaries), the two protagonists of the drug war—the Mafia and the police—are, in a strictly economic sense, each others' best friends. They both build and strengthen each other's business.

SUCCESSFUL MAFIA, WEAKER SOCIETY

The failure of drug control by police repression is more than just a failure to attain a stated objective. It also makes for a serious drain on the economic strength of American society—both by rendering the problem worse in itself and by causing high costs in handling the problem. The damage to society from the enforcement system is direct by the increased effects of the drugs on the population. Especially the extension of street pushing into many school yards is an odiously destructive intrusion where it hurts society the most, and this intrusion would be much less likely to happen if the drug trade had not been strengthened by the ineffectual enforcement system.

The indirect effects of the ineffectual drug laws are even worse. For one thing, it makes organized crime a much larger force in American society than it would be otherwise. Its muscle is felt far outside the drug problem as such. Threats of wildcat strikes, unless demands for illegal cash payments are met, increase the cost overruns in such sensitive areas as defense contracts and power station construction. When organized crime continues to infiltrate legitimate business, to use such firms as fronts and as tax accounts for illegal incomes, then this contributes to lowering the efficiency of businesses used in these ways.

In still another way, the ineffectual drug law enforcement system weakens law enforcement in general, by taking up a great deal of time in the courts and by contributing to overcrowding in the prisons; ultimately it makes the prison system larger than it need be. Drug users should not really be society's first priority to keep out of circulation. How many robbers are now paroled too early because the cells are needed for recently convicted individuals found guilty of "possession"? Equally bad is the relativizing of the concept of crime. The absurdity of trying to punish all the technically criminal drug users—an estimated ten million Americans smoke marijuana—leads to "selective" law enforcement which of course is the opposite of equal justice under the law and weakens the public's trust in the legal system.

This tangle of interlocking damages to society makes one wonder, who keeps this system in place? It is no secret that Mafia agents acted as lobbyists against the repeal of Prohibition, in the early 1930's. It is greatly to be suspected that current organized criminals do likewise, and so do probably some of their relatives who occupy sheltered positions as technically legitimate heirs to criminally amassed fortunes. When such underground forces join together with the super-moralists of the political system, then politics has indeed brought together some strange bedfellows. Another element in the coalition may be a tendency to focus "selective enforcement" on people from minorities and urban ghettos, as a form of racial and cultural persecution. Such alliances will not be broken until public opinion has become enlightened enough to demand an end to this extreme form of social waste.

A ROAD TO SANITY: EDUCATION

A common denominator of systems which have handled drug problems better than what goes on in America is that they focus on the underlying causes rather than the surface phenomenon of drug abuse. The craving for intoxication comes from a yearning for release from life's pressures and frustrations. The real solution must be found in education in the wide sense—cultural broadening supplying mental stimuli which reinforce the individual's will to live with a clear mind. By contrast, the so-called drug culture also looks at the problem the wrong way: drugs can not expand the mind, they merely undermine, draining its energies.

In any event, less repressive systems have had better results. England has a record of treating heroine addiction as an illness, with the drug available to *bona fide* addicts on prescription, at a low price. With such a dispensation, addicts have no motive either for robbery or for recruiting new addicts.

On alcohol control also, some countries have better results from high taxation. This generates revenue for the public, by which to police the system. The wages of sin go to society at large rather than to the underworld. Illegal trade can also be controlled better when it does not have the support of numerous addicts making common cause with the crooks against the authorities.

In a positive sense we know from Scandinavia, for example, that the best way to combat alcoholism is in the sports—not the spectator sports but participation sports in which large numbers of people become motivated to excel. Other aspects of deepening mass education also have paid off in more sobriety. By contrast, the steadily worsening alcoholism problem in the Soviet Union testifies to the effect of boredom which even an accomplished police state can not handle.

Saying "education" can easily be misunderstood, however. As we shall see, the existing school systems often prepare for the boredom and the lack of personal motivation which are essential background for the drug problem as well as for other forms of social waste.

Chapter 7
Schoolroom Boredom and Pop Entertainment

Education is many things to many people. How disappointed we are over its results will depend on what we were expecting. The current crisis of confidence in formal education in America includes the usual paradox of social waste: people are disappointed, not because the system has failed but because the results are in fact what should have been expected from the system. On the whole, we get what we bargained for. The question is, how many people understand, or reflect on, what they are bargaining for? Let us reflect on the purposes of formal schooling.

The school system, as it exists, includes several objectives which are in latent or open conflict with each other. In descending order of their human worth, these objectives may be listed as (1) developing the full intellectual and/or aesthetic potential of each individual; (2) imparting society's values, habits and tacit assumptions; (3) training for specific, economically useful skills; (4) training for obedience, self-restraint and social discipline; and (5) babysitting.

Cutting across some of these objectives are the techniques of applied education: by spontaneous initiative or by more or less constraining inducement, and by individual efforts or through a collectivized setting. Education can, further, be pupil centered, classroom centered, teacher centered, textbook centered, or vaguely unfocused.

This jumble of purposes and approaches will largely decide the degree of failure in the educational system. Make no mistake about it: most education is a failure from several viewpoints and entails vast amounts of social waste. As long as we put up with education as it is, we have few grounds to complain about its immediate results, or about its continuation into the shallowness of modern mass culture.

THE TRIBAL SCHOOL

In pre-modern cultures there was not much organized teaching. The young were imparted the culture and the social values of their elders, mainly by being among them. As long as the local culture changed but slowly, almost imperceptibly, there was no need to organize teaching as a separate profession or even as a separate activity. In a near-static culture, everybody was an expert on that culture, and everyone was a qualified teacher. Thus, families taught their own offspring, and the young were exposed to the collective wisdom of the tribe in a variety of ways, in daily work and play, at festivities and ceremonies. Everyone was taught, even though few if any knew that they were being taught. Emphasis was on imparting society's values etc. and on learning its economically relevant skills. In a traditional, slow-moving setting, reading and writing were unnecessary, arithmetic of very limited application.

The primary reason for organized schools has always been the need to teach things which the family and the tribe were unable to handle. China's mandarins, Mediaeval Europe's priests and lawyers etc., had to learn things which were not in the mental baggage of the families from which most of the candidates came. (In Mediaeval Europe, this was especially true of the priesthood for they had—officially—no offspring at all). Practical arts and crafts were usually learned "on the job", in formal or informal apprenticeship.

Gradually, as society's need for specialized skills became larger, the demand for formal schooling also grew. The day came when society's changes had become so rapid that parents and other tribal relatives no longer could handle all the teaching of new material that came along. The modern, universal primary school came into being, mainly during the last 150 years or so, as a consequence of the realization that all children needed to know reading and writing because they also needed to learn things which are beyond the capacity of the tribe to teach them, and which therefore have to be conveyed in written form.

None of this prevents the tribe from continuing to function, above all in the molding of character and basic values of the time and place. Only it is not the old tribe any more: community, social stratum, neighborhood, even age-peer groups do to children—and not only in pre-school ages—what the old tribes once did.

When the school fails, some of the failure comes from not realizing what the tribe has taught. The recent conflict about testing teachers is an example; it overlooked how often black Americans (for instance) are differently trained by the subculture in which they receive their before-school training.

The traditional tribal school, in its time, was the only school which was clearly successful, for traditional society used to be of one mind. In modern schools the objectives have become separated from each other and from the over-all objectives of the society, which is no longer of one mind—the unity of purpose is no longer there.

THE LIBERAL IDEAL

"Developing the whole person" sounds like as high an ideal as anyone could cherish, and it should be all in line with the American principle of individualism—or is it? Individual potential is best realized when the individual works individually, without undue constraints by collectives, by teachers, or by imposed routines. The annals of education contain some shining case histories of individual attainment in an aristocratic setting where elite pupils were allowed to approach their study material with a maximum of individual incentive.

Such ideals are a negative reflection on organized mass education. They reflect the finding that no one can really teach anyone anything that the pupils are not about to learn by themselves. The teachers, then, are of secondary significance at best, or may often be a positive nuisance if they are too ignorant, too arrogant, or too dull to allow the pupils to learn.

This may be the basic reason for the recent rash toward "unschooling" in America. Parents who are disenchanted with organized schools take their children out of school and undertake to educate them at home by their own efforts—or, in fact, mainly by the children's efforts when they are less hamstrung by uncongenial surroundings.

Anyone who has been through this kind of experience can testify to both the advantages and the drawbacks of such a system of learning. There is no doubt that learning in solitude or privacy is more productive than any classroom setting can hope to be normally. There are of course exceptions to all rules, but you don't build systems on exceptions. Without dull or envious comrades to disturb the bright child, and free from uncomprehending teachers interfering with a child's intellectual processes at the wrong moment, it is far easier to concentrate on the material to be learned. There is also more flexibility between good and bad days, and more allowance can be made for the coming and going of moods which are conducive sometimes to active learning and sometimes to digesting material already learned.

The driving force must be individual interest in the materials. Intellectual guidance by teachers, parents or others is mainly in the choice of curriculum and books. Learning to read can be done in quite a short time when the child is offered things to read which capture the imagination and the intellect of an early age, rather than the dull "readers" composed according to pedagogic theory. Learning a foreign language, as soon as the mother tongue is firmly entrenched, is also greatly expedited if it is approached without the linguists' hangup about formal grammar. *Simplicissimus*, the German humor magazine, many years ago had a cartoon showing a middle aged, rather abstract schoolteacher and his equally unprepossessing wife, both contemplating their five-year-old son who could not speak even his mother tongue despite incessant instruction in German grammar. When approached like a mother tongue, even a foreign language can be absorbed by letting the child loose on an engaging book, with a dictionary as main instruction and occasionally some sound recordings for pronunciation. Grammar can be filled in later, to rationalize why the foreign phrases are the way they are. And so it goes with the gamut of school subjects: mathematics, natural sciences, geography, history etc. are all learned faster when they are allowed to help the individual comprehend what goes on in the world.

None of this means that the pupil is given a free hand to engage only in subjects that appear to be fun to begin with. There have to be organized curricula to lay down what it is that has to be learned, and in what proportions and sequences. But given this precondition, individual study is normally, and by a large margin, the most efficient method of acquiring knowledge.

Against this ideal of individual fulfilment stands the organized school as a socializer and as a disciplinary and babysitting organization. Studying all by one's self leaves too little room for acquiring the attitudes which will be necessary if the individual is to cooperate with others in real life, a condition more compelling than ever in today's high-technology world which demands interdependence and teamwork at all levels, between individuals and groups as well as between nations.

This dichotomy—socializing versus knowledge—is in itself enough to call in question the more extreme ways of individual education such as "unschooling". Over-riding this dichotomy, however, is the practical impossibility of organizing all or most of the education of the masses in this manner. In our modern world, few people have retained the teaching abilities of the traditional tribal school; they have retained those abilities mainly in regard to the common tacit assumptions of their own parochial world. Equally important, most parents nowadays do not have the time to supervise their children's schoolwork. It is true of course that the individual method is so productive that it does not have to take all day. But after a full day in a factory or an office, and with all the strain in commuting and shopping, most parents today do not have enough strength to check their children's homework in the evening. By the arguments developed in other chapters of this book, some of these strains of modern life might be less fatiguing if things like commuting and shopping were organized differently from what is usually the case. But even so, it is unlikely that parents' time would normally be sufficient to do more than perfunctory checks on what the children have done with several hours of schoolwork. Many parents are single nowadays, and many married couples hold two jobs. Thus the family no longer can supply the manpower, the time, or the strength to supervise the children's studies—this quite apart from the fact that many parents have not themselves mastered all of the curriculum the children are to go through. School should teach knowledge which is up-to-date at the time, and many parents are behind the times or not sufficiently educated themselves. Enter the professional teacher, rendered even more indispensable by the babysitting function of the school system.

SCHOOLROOM COLLECTIVE

In the schoolroom, the children meet their age peers. That would be good if these peers represent a cross section of contemporary society. Much of the time they do not. In some contrast to the Old World, American society is class stratified by areas of residence. The socializing value of collective schooling is hampered by the pseudo conservative concept of the "neighborhood school" which trains for ghetto partisanship rather than for national citizenship. The same constraint on socializing is further buttressed by the "parent-teacher association", a grouping often designed to hamstring the teachers, to prevent them from doing their job which is giving the children what the parents can not give them. Neighborhoods in America tend to be rather homogenous, in income above all, and in ethnicity and subculture often as well. Such homogeneity is reinforced by the ease of automobile transportation. Thus, children in school risk to be exposed only to the same socially distorting influences as at home. Once more, rapid transportation turns out to be a convenient means of not getting anywhere except physically. Minds can be immobilized because nothing forces the exposure which can only come from being immobilized (physically) together with people of different background. The urgent need for social integration is frustrated or delayed by the way economic affluence is used to build walls around the children of the privileged.

Social homogeneity in the school can only worsen the negative effects of peer pressure. Up to a point peer pressure is a necessary element in the socialization of the child, but when this means reinforcement of parochial social norms the result is largely negative. Peer pressure in the school, all too often, becomes a pressure for conformity and mediocrity, and hostile toward individual excellence. "Teachers' pets" are often ill treated by comrades in school. Eager beavers are forced back to class conformity.

Class conformism has some positive features. One of these is the enforcing of standard language which is a precondition for standard spelling, for instance; both are necessary for people functioning in an economy relying on both spoken and written language.

But in a narrowly parochial setting this means parochial usage, group slang and other means of continuing the cleavage against other classes in society as well as against other regional accents. Class conformism emphasizes mediocrity, especially in intellectual subjects, while hero worship is reserved for physical exploits, above all those aiming at stardom in the spectator sports with their crude community appeal. In more extreme forms, class conformism encourages gangs and hooligan groups; it makes easier the access to drugs (pushed in schools because the profit is so high under repression) and makes more frequent the irresponsible use of sex. A general effect is to heighten peer solidarity at the expense of the cohesion with the rest of society which schools are supposed to foster. The schoolroom collective in many cases becomes a schoolroom jungle which many parents fear, and for good reason.

In its crude way, the problem of schoolroom conformism points to one of the basic dilemmas of all organized education: that education is supposed to foster conforming social attitudes (in the interest of communication and social cohesion) and the acquisition of knowledge, both at the same time. Now these two purposes are to a large extent at odds with each other. Maximize knowledge and you foster oddballs, not team players. Maximize team spirit, and you remove large parts of all possible knowledge, above all those parts which point forward to new knowledge, innovation in all areas of human endeavor. We have to reflect on this dichotomy in education. It may help us understand why so many American top level scientists and artists are foreign born. For the moment, let us pursue the dilemma into the classroom itself, a place which emphasizes one's being in a group when learning.

CLASSROOM TEACHING IS LOW PRODUCTIVE

We have pointed it out already: individuals learn faster when they do it individually, without collective constraints. Even when teaching University undergraduates, one is struck by an elementary and depressing observation: during a large part of the class hour, the class as a whole sits and listens when the dumbest among them say it wrong. This can be worse than nothing, for there is always the risk of learning the wrong answer just by listening to it—once it has been committed to memory it is frequently mistaken for the right answer. The only escape from listening to dumb answers, as I am told by former high-school students, is not to listen at all. Thus time is lost, pent-up initiatives are frustrated. The result of classroom sitting becomes very little, generally in inverse proportion to the size of the class. Very little positively, that is; but quite a lot negatively by frustration, loss of interest in what goes on in the class.

The main exception to the low productivity of classroom work is in very small classes, as for instance of graduate students not exceeding ten at a time who may all be focussing on the same problem at the same time. But this is an elite case and covers a very small part of the whole educational establishment. Even then, the teacher (if reflecting on it) can not help being haunted by a chilling thought: bright students do not need a teacher, only educated company. The face-to-face setting of classical British tutoring is the most efficient form of instruction, but it is evidently not to be applied to mass education. In any event, it is the marginal students who need teachers the most, and they need them the more, the closer to failure they are. A large part of what a teacher does consists in helping students who in the end become workers of dubious quality in whatever positions which their diplomas get them.

Classroom teaching not only is low productive if we compare the input of time and effort with the output of knowledge helped along by it. It also produces some outputs of questionable benefit—to society as well as to individuals. With less schooling, the low-quality intellects would not clutter up the work places with their diplomas. They might be of more adequate quality for the positions to which a lower level of formal competence will assign them. Those who are more competent would then also face fewer obstacles on their way to positions where their abilities are sorely needed. The next chapter will elaborate on this theme in connection with discrimination by sex, "race" etc.

There is a German saying that "reading makes stupid". Formal learning beyond one's intellectual reach becomes counter productive. Too much of it can also be a positive obstacle. Some recent critics have charged that American schools fail to teach their charges to think. This is stating it much too mildly. To a large extent, schools actively prevent children from thinking on their own.

The over-all effects of today's diploma mills contain many negative results. In my parents' and grandparents' time, there were many individuals with no more than six weeks of formal schooling who went far in their careers on the basis of native intelligence and essential character. In my time, I have known individuals with advanced academic degrees who were not fit for any work at all.

THE MORE THE WORSE

As the education debate now is flaring high, many of the past failures get reflected in the kind of proposals being made to improve the system. Among the new remedies are more classroom hours and more homework at the same time.

As to more classroom hours, how could this be brought about without having even more teachers at work? Of all countries in the world, America has among the highest ratios of teachers to total work force, around 4 percent. The problem is analogous to that of the police: to recruit even larger numbers, we would have to recruit from even lower strata of intelligence, character and general competence. The problem of quality of teaching is not merely one of being stuck with too many pupils who do not want to study but are there because their families would not know what to do with them if they were not in school. It is also a problem of quality of teachers in a society where high income levels make teachers expensive. There are limits as to how much society wants to spend on the school system.

The problem of teacher quality was illustrated for us some years ago when the junior-college system came into being, in rather short order. It was intended originally to provide practical training in trades for which the economy has a demand, to youngsters who generally had not done well enough in high school to be admitted to universities. The quality of American high-school graduates is often so low that the junior colleges had to become, in effect, remedial high schools. To build up the system in a few years, it was inevitable that the junior colleges would attract as teachers many of the best among existing high-school teachers, or their immediately prospective replacements. Thus, just by being there, the junior colleges contributed to lowering the average quality of the high-school teaching staffs. It should have been no surprise that this led to even lower quality of high-school graduates. By the usual inverted logic of social waste, this led to the appearance of an even larger need for the kinds of education which the junior colleges offer—even to turn out acceptable secretaries and specialty-store clerks. Thus a virtual redundancy, the junior college as a remedial high school, created its own seeming justification. The obvious solution would have been to improve the high schools, not by making them larger but by raising their standards of both admission and of graduation. This would have caused less social waste. It was not proposed with much authority. Those in a position to take the high-level decisions, whether they were in politics or in the higher ranks of the educational establishment, saw instead their vested interest in maintaining the wastefulness of the system. Like the white bread, the too many automobiles and the drug police, the social waste in education also employs people; it absorbs some resources which therefore are paid at higher rates.

Requiring more classroom hours will only magnify the failures of the past. Throwing more money at the school system, without profound system change, will be as self defeating as the drug enforcement system.

FILL THE TIME, WASTE THE TALENT

End-of-school cartoons depict the horror of the housewife who dreads the prospect of having unruly offspring hanging around the home—or perhaps loitering in the streets—all day for two-and-a-half months. If school were not there to begin with, it would have been invented as a means of keeping the children away during all the time when the parents can not or will not cope with them. At the same time, labor statisticians are toiling with "seasonal adjustments" of the data on unemployment, especially that of teenagers which typically gets worse during the summer. The children's time is there to waste, the economy does not want them, and neither do their parents; so what is the harm in the social waste of their time?

The answer is that wasting of talent does not end with the school year. When the children have been taught counter-productive attitudes toward work and life, these attitudes will stay with them, often for life. Seen from that angle, the social waste is enormous.

The educational professions, for their part, have not been idle in trying to find means of making the schools' low-productive use of time appear meaningful. Teaching texts are often made as dull as possible, composed as they are by mechanistic quasi-science rather than by empathetic insights into the needs of young minds. The cases of "look-say" reading and "new math" are among the most telling, and the recent drive for more computer work (before the children have learned to understand what it is that the computers compute) is a naked case of "supply-side" waste—the goods have to be consumed because they have been produced.

"Look-say" reading systems may not be as popular as they once were. All told, they were one of the most pathetic mistakes made anywhere by any profession. In brief, the system tried to disregard the simple fact of the alphabet's twenty-six letters. Instead the children's attention was directed to whole syllables and how they resembled those in words which had nothing in common except those groups of letters. The examples are too silly to repeat. There can be no doubt whatsoever that the net result of look-say reading instruction was to retard the learning, and eventually the whole mental development, of millions of children. How this pseudo-educational monstrosity was ever put together, let alone given any credence, defies the imagination. In "underdeveloped" countries, there are cases on record of adults who learned reading in the course of an afternoon.

The "new math" is yet another case of intellectual-technological overkill. Whatever its mathematical merits, it did more harm than good in elementary teaching because it attempted to disregard the natural sense of numbers which we all learn very early (unless someone prevents it). How elementary this sense is becomes clear when people who once changed their language are found to count, in their minds, with the numerals of the mother tongue—this happens even with advanced intellectuals such as Marie Curie.

As to the premature teaching of computer skills, it may be enough to point out that much of what video-computers do, in weird (pseudo) science fiction games, is in fact the old well-known war games, really no different from chess or tic-tac-to. Doing it electronically may seem more fun, until the novelty becomes old hat; and when that happens we will be worse off, not better, for having made simple things look complicated.

ANTHILL DRILL VERSUS MENTAL UNFOLDING

The dilemma of school discipline preventing children from learning rather than helping them is not unique to America. But it has come to extremes here because the high ambitions of mass education were combined with the pervasive tendency toward social waste in disposing of the fruits of affluence.

To say that mass education prevents learning more than it helps is no exaggeration. The depth of mental repression through education has only begun to be gauged here and there. The normal individual, endowed with a brain free of physical defects and with normal physical strength is, in fact, a potential genius. We have no reason to wish for higher birthrates in order that we may have more geniuses. Developing those we already have around ourselves is already more than we can handle.

This point explains, among other things, the old riddle about a connection between genius and insanity. The mentally defective would tend to escape some of the conforming pressures of society and thus to retain unscathed more of the potential which is educated away in most of us. Other kinds of exceptional endowment can have the same paradoxically liberating effect. Leonardo da Vinci was a motherless homosexual. Aldous Huxley and Eric Hoffer both grew up functionally blind, thus protected from much of the formal and informal schooling of their age. Babies rendered severely malformed by their mothers' use of the drug Thalidomide (supposed to be harmless, from animal experiments) during pregnancy—many such babies without arms and legs show a mental alertness which indirectly testifies to the depressing effects of normal education at all levels.

Education as a mental depressant is easily visualized in the conditions of economic penury which have been with our species during most of its existence, at least since the invention of organized agriculture. Good government in old theocratic or bureaucratic states such as Egypt and Babylonia, Inca Peru, and Imperial China, all had in common the single-minded teaching of obedience and of simple agricultural skills which were necessary if large numbers of people were to live at the same time. This was in ages when the toil of the farmers was low productive and allowed of only a very small surplus to feed the priests and rulers who had to be few and who must live quite differently from the masses. The picture resembles that of an anthill or a beehive where most members are starvation dwarfs serving a small number of complete individuals, the queens and drones. In imperial Russia, the peasant was known by a term which means "little man", "homunculus". He was not supposed to be a whole man, either mentally or maybe even physically. Through the ages, color bias has also worked against the underfed peons who often became darker because of undernourishment no less than by working in the heat of the open field. We have expressions of this all the way from Arabian Nights ("a face like the full moon" suggested extreme beauty) to some boondocks in rural India where very dark "aboriginals" are still looked down upon by the more normally brown.

Democracy was supposed to turn all this around. It should want citizens with independent judgment, not well rounded yes-men. Even democracy has its elites, if for no other reason so because "positional goods" (the value of being in leadership position or in the limelight) are rationed by the very logic of things. To loosen up the constraints which enforced "peasant stupidity" (stupidity, that is, of matters which were not part of a peasant's own sphere of work and thought) requires economic affluence, yes, but it also requires that affluence be used intelligently and not squandered in the organized social waste of "supply-side" school systems.

"Positional goods" apart, many people may have an instinctual fear of a world in which most of the potential geniuses are fully developed. If it happened in short order, the explosion of knowledge, insight, and initiative could easily blow up the entire social order and land us into complete chaos. So, whatever is done to upgrade education to make it more of a development of individual minds and less a one-sided training for routine workers, the transition has to be gradual. But making it slower than is necessary for tolerable continuity risks leading us back to a new kind of anthill training—one where the masses are trained to demand the fruits of mass goods industry because they are there and must be consumed rather than because they serve human purposes. A look at the cultural scene will explain how bad mass education generates bad mass culture feeding back into continued bad mass education, and so on.

FROM CONFORMISM TO VULGARITY

This transition is a paradox, for some degree of conformity is necessary even for individual development. To function, even for our own purposes, we must be able to communicate. This requires standard language to the point of uniform spelling, homogenous grammatical conventions, and so on. With chaos in language there would be no communication, hence no affluence and no real freedom either. Learning the parameters of the culture is necessary if one is to move freely within it. But to be confined within only those parameters makes one parochial, unable to move about in other cultures and, in effect, narrowly restricted within the parochial culture, thus without any real freedom.

The question then is, since we have to conform up to a point, what is that point? In America, the pressure on immigrants to conform to the prevailing strictures of immediate surroundings has been so strong that the immigrants' grandchildren often lost the ability to communicate in more ways than the one parochial way which was enforced upon them. Faced with foreign languages the response then, all too often, is the "just can't learn" of the Army wife abroad. Thus the implicit promise of the "melting pot" of becoming a prototype for a future world of cosmopolitans was lost. Small nations, in fact, appear to do better at true internationalism.

Language was cited here as the simplest prototype of culture. Forced conformity in other spheres of culture lowers the level of literary and aesthetic perceptions. Only this can explain the popularity of television soap operas, or of the seemingly contrasting (but complementary) genres of "romance" novels produced on the assembly lines and of rank pornography. Neither of these suit people who are adult in any real sense. So what has education produced here? Both the "romances" and the pornography might as well be written by computers and lightly overhauled by "re-writing squads" as in Orwell's *1984*. The habit of low productive learning in school leads to a lifetime habit of low productive pastimes.

The mystery of it is that free enterprise society in America tends to generate as much conformism as that which Communism tries to enforce in Russia. Perhaps even more so, because the pressures of a society ruled by money are more built-in and less easily identified: our golden rule seems to be that "he who owns the gold, makes the rules". Under the supply-side waste of our economy and our educational system, the young are so over supplied with cues and messages both in and out of school that many of them build up defenses and refuse even to listen. Communist conformism, by contrast, is so obvious that many individuals resist it by clamming up, retiring into their inner private life to which the propaganda is too clumsy to reach. We have no opinion polls to back up this conclusion, but one indication is that many Russians are clinging with remarkable tenacity to the sophisticated literature of their pre-socialist past, a habit which may maintain more articulate speech than is found among Americans nurtured on "reading matter" which was concocted to fit their mental level rather than to raise it.

The circle closes itself, because when school conformism leads to vulgar conformism in cultural tastes, it also sets the quality standard from which we can recruit teachers as well as other cadres which are essential to the functioning of a democratic society. It is rather remarkable that there are as many competent, self reliant characters in our society as there actually are. Obviously, conformism in a free society has loopholes, maybe as many as those of the tax system. The many small failures of school regimentation add up to the saving grace of the system and prevent the complete debacle of a culture that one might have expected from the analysis given above.

So, where do we go from here? Between the extremes of schoolroom boredom and complete, anarchic "unschooling", how can we formulate a more productive system of education which can mobilize more of the squandered riches of the mind without blowing the social fabric to pieces?

A SHIFT OF EMPHASIS

A more productive school system should no doubt include less classroom sitting and more individual study. In order not to make this sound impossible, let us imagine a school with larger reading rooms attached to its library. There would be regular reading hours keyed to specified subjects and even specified central texts. Some of the less successful classroom teachers could then instead serve as supervisors, to see to it that order and decorum prevail in the reading rooms and among the carrells or booths for instrument use. They would also see to it that the required texts do receive the intended attention. The better teachers would as before supervise the results of learning, both by traditional class hours and by individual checks on what the charges have learned.

Such a division of labor between reading supervisors and real teachers could also dissolve the conflict about merit pay for teachers. Instead, there would be fewer teachers employed as such. Their pay could then be better than it is now when teacher pay is extended to too many people.

Besides books, there will of course also be other "teaching aids" (or, should we say, "learning aids"?) such as films and sound recordings. Video material should go a long way in conveying (to grade school and high school students) the essentials of experimental science, and at a fraction of the cost of live laboratories which could then be kept at a minimum.

The main emphasis on the library may appear old fashioned, but the long and the short of the experience from several decades of toying with teaching machines is and remains the fact that the printed book is the most efficient teaching machine that anyone has yet invented. It allows on the whole a much more flexible and versatile relation between learner and text than is found in the more recent forms of instructional material. And of course the library would also be the place where the film and cassette material would be kept. Reading booths to study such material would also be part of the reading room system and subject to its discipline. That discipline would be designed to secure both the time and the undisturbed access to individual study and to enforce much more individual work than happens now.

As already mentioned, no one can teach anyone anything that the pupils are not about to learn by their own efforts. This places less importance with the classroom teacher but so much the more so with the textbook writer. The real "master teacher" is the person who writes first-rate instructional text, or designs first-rate recorded lessons. From those, young minds may learn, leaving live teachers to fill in gaps and check the accuracy and completeness of learning. Moving the emphasis back to the mind that learns will also free us from the stereotype of teaching as force feeding; school children should not be treated like French geese. The starting point must be in their own mental appetites and these can not be created artificially. Nor is that necessary; it is quite enough if these appetites are not destroyed by meaningless "classroom activity" reflecting more or less mechanistic constructs of educational psychology.

Would such a school system cost more than at present, or less, or the same? That, obviously, depends on how much we decide to spend on it. Whatever that level, the return to dollars spent will be immeasurably larger—beyond measure, indeed, for the aim is to develop young minds. To waste young minds is a terrible thing to do.

Chapter 8
Discrimination and the Waste of Talent

The waste of talent through education is basic and pervasive. It gets even worse because of the discriminations in our society which continue despite all efforts to do away with them. The largest is sex discrimination, which places half of the population at a disadvantage. Next comes discrimination by "race" (a misnomer for subculture), and by "social origin" which in this country is mainly a euphemism for the differences in coaching between the children of the rich, the well-to-do, and the poor.

Equal rights are an ethical issue and could be argued on that plane alone. They are more than that, however: they also bear on the national economy. The ethical point, that discrimination is wrong, has been made many times and rightly so; but it does not appear to carry enough weight in the real world to force the changes which most of us agree should be made. The economic consequences of discrimination are seldom spelled out in full. If they were more commonly understood, maybe we would see more forceful action for equal rights, including their enshrining in the Constitution where they obviously belong. It is time to develop the economic theme in some detail.

A MATTER OF FAIR COMPETITION

In a nutshell, it is this: Whenever a mediocre white man gets a job which a bright woman or minority man can do better, society is shortchanged, for we are then less well served. Productivity is lower under discrimination. This goes also for discrimination on the basis of social origin, the counterpart of which is nepotism. All discrimination is made easier by the educational system when it gives the mediocre white men access to formal competence which they can not quite live up to.

This capsule formulation has several facets. First, there is the technical competence to perform specified tasks, and the underlying gift or native ability to acquire such competence. This need becomes more urgent year by year because the tasks in a modern, high-technology economic system become more and more exacting as to the precise character and quality of competence for each task, including among them the managerial tasks which have turned out to be very important in a modern economy. Second, there is the human competence of exercising leadership—in industry, civic affairs, politics, the military, and so on—in an unbiased way, as only unbiased people can; and this too has economic consequences both direct and indirect. Third, there is the need for all kinds of talent and all kinds of cultural orientation to "fill the bill" of a modern society. Finally, the competitive drive which is essential in a modern economy is sure to be blunted under discrimination, both among those favored by the discrimination and those wronged by it. Competition is needed more than ever when many of those traditionally favored by discrimination no longer keep up, their drive blunted by disillusionment, drug abuse, and the failure of industrial society to explain itself to all its members as well as its failure always to put performance above group loyalties and social classifications.

TECHNICAL COMPETENCE

Discrimination against women and minorities has long been supported by pseudo evidence on purported differences in native ability, between the sexes and between the "races". Usually, such evidence crumbles when exposed to critical scrutiny: the statistics have been biased by the results of past discrimination. When women and minorities are kept away from some of the tasks which society rewards with high incomes, both of them develop subcultures which place the average woman and the average minority person at a disadvantage. This is because competition for the admission to advanced training, and to the positions such training leads to, has been systematically tailored to the cultural equipment of white men. Thus discrimination was made to justify itself. The loss to society, in the meantime, has been immense, the social waste unfathomable.

Whenever the testing for native ability is done in a way that eliminates the effects of past discrimination, the purported superiority of white men usually evaporates. But even so, the question is incorrectly stated when made to refer to statistical averages. The evidence about brilliance in many women, and in many minority men, is so overwhelming that we can safely throw the averages in the waste basket. Testing for individual ability is necessary in any event, and it is all that is needed or justified.

The rising need for trained talent in modern society stands in sharp contrast with the class formation which took place in pre-industrial times, from the Bronze Age to the 1800's. We already touched on some of this from the angle of education. In the old days of chronic penury which resulted from slow moving technology and from population growth restricted only by the "malthusian checks" (hunger, sickness, war, etc.), society's leaders saw an important purpose to keep most people faithfully to the drudgery of their low-technology economic system. Peasant society with its low productive food farming needed to tie nearly all hands to the soil. Latent brain power threatened to get in the way unless it was trained into mindless submission. The need for and the use of high talent was so small that it could without difficulty be filled from the ranks of the privileged. So it went in Babylon and Rome and Inca Peru, in baroque Europe and Imperial China. In early industrial society (e.g., England at the time of Marx) most factory tasks were simple routines, easily learned. Workers could easily be replaced by hiring strike breakers from among the unemployed in the street. Even in Babbitt's America (Sinclair Lewis), the leaders of industry did what they could to see to it that the ranks of the industrial army were taught no more than "they would need" in order to serve a productive system which they were not supposed to control. Only in the last fifty to seventy-five years have specialized skills begun to dominate the economic scene. Only recently have equal rights had a fighting chance.

Such antecedents may help explain the class and category thinking which still lingers on, and perhaps mostly among people who describe themselves as "conservatives". But that justifies nothing. Rigid classes always were evil from a human viewpoint. They always meant some social waste compared with more systematic recruiting of outstanding talent wherever it might be found. In a society of penury, such social waste was relatively less striking than it is in a society which holds affluence among its options. America prides itself of being the land of opportunity. Why then is there so much emotional resistance against granting that opportunity to all who deserve it? There is some progress, but there are also telling cases of retrogression, worsening discrimination, in the early and mid 1900's. For instance, much of the construction work in American cities (the South above all, for obvious reasons) used to rely on the work of black brickmakers and construction workers. More recently, blacks were muscled out of the building trades unions—on the face of it, to ensure quality of workmanship. The incipient re-admission of black workers into such trades confirms what was in fact known beforehand, that they are able to produce excellent workmanship. The pretext of "quality" was false all along, there never was any excuse for it. It merely secured higher wages to white workers because their skills were more scarce under discrimination. The consequences included higher costs and social waste.

Discrimination against women also took a turn for the worse in the wave of retrogression that followed upon the end of World War 2. During the war, women had done a great deal of the often skilled and exacting factory work to produce weapons and other necessities of war. But thereafter they were to a large extent nudged out of work places they had proved themselves competent to handle; systematically they were relegated to low paying jobs and home work. Thus the "feminine mystique" (Betty Friedan) was exploited to reduce women into less complete human beings, and to over-reward the work of barely competent males. It is not by mere coincidence that this took place in the 1950's, the same period when the political regime made the decisive mistakes in resource policy.

Disdain for women's capabilities often goes to ridiculous extremes. Not long ago, a senior animal scientist in this country was heard saying that he would not entrust his milk cows to the care of women! He must have lost all touch with his North European origins where dairy farming always was predominantly women's work—including the exacting and dangerous summer stays on mountain outfarms without any male protection.

Against absurdities of this type, reason and compassion have an uphill fight. The main support for equality of rights comes in fact from the increasing complexity of the work place itself. How far modern industry has been transformed since the days of Karl Marx is evident whenever we see a major strike. No longer can factory owners recruit strike breakers from among the unemployed in the street. The specialized crews who operate steel mills, machine shops, power stations, and countless other complex productive and service facilities, can not be replaced at short notice. We had a fresh example not long ago: the firing of numerous air traffic controllers which meant reducing immediately, by one-fourth, of the system of civil aviation. Replacement controllers can be recruited and trained only over several years.

The difficulty of replacing of skilled workers places a floor under pay scales as no labor union can do. Pay scales relate to employers' risks: the more capital and production that is associated with each employee, the greater the risk to the firm of hiring and retaining someone not fully on the level of the task. Higher productivity requires unbiased recruitment to secure standards. Cohesion of groups already on the job such as "closed-shop" unions who prevent or retard equal rights, then also reduce productivity, keep it lower than it might be.

Allowing equal rights and equal opportunity in this complex economic world means higher quality manpower, other things being equal. It also means applying a concept much in the news recently: "supply-side" economics. This concept is often dubious in the way it is advanced as a tool in national economic policy, because it is generally made to relate only to funds for investment without tying in with other factors of production and their supply. Granting women and minorities full access to the work place and its rewards, and to the training opportunities leading there, represents in fact the best possible application of supply-side economics. Quality manpower, in improved quality (because of increased competition between individuals) and at somewhat lower cost (because competition increases its supply) would be a powerful booster to the whole economic system and its productivity. It would mean more, in fact, than is now claimed (in rather unclear terms) for the purported increase in funds for investment which has been expected from lowering the income tax. So far, the claim in favor of Federal tax relief as an incentive to increase real investment had not been supported by events.

It seems, rather, that the money which individuals no longer pay as income tax reverts to the Federal treasury as borrowing. It looks like an ironic case of over rating purely financial manipulations. In the social sphere, we have been told for years, and with considerable emphasis, problems are not solved just by throwing money at them. Why would that be more likely on industrial problems? The economy suffers from structural imbalances chiefly in energy and capital supply. Discrimination still adds substantially to these imbalances. Correcting for that does not have to cost much money. It only costs the reinforcing of our sense of justice with a better awareness of the economic damage caused by discrimination. Economically, the payoff from equal rights will be high.

The same applies to the military. Our high-technology war machine is in urgent need of all the best talent it can get if it is to produce full value for the expensive hardware. It is naive to point to foxhole fighting as a reason to exclude women from combat service. Very little of the fighting in a modern war takes place in foxholes anyway. And the limit between combat and non-combat duties is more and more blurred; for instance, in World War 2, British anti-aircraft batteries used drafted young women as "spotters"—they killed German airmen as surely as did the men who pulled the triggers on the guns. In America, women with medical competence are already now subject to the draft. Their physical danger will often be about the same as that of the combat troops—unlike support personnel they can not be kept very far away from where the shooting is. Make no mistake about the future role of women in combat: what the military leadership requests, Congress will grant, whether it runs one way or the other. What the Constitution says or fails to say about civil rights has very little to do with military service, because bearing arms on behalf of the country is a matter of civic duty, not primarily of civil rights. Recent Supreme Court decisions have confirmed the conclusion which comes out of careful study of the old Constitution itself: that the military system is to a large extent exempt from the rules on constitutional civil rights. In war, military reality will reign supreme. A woman who is a crack fighter pilot will go into combat whenever this makes a difference to the outcome of the battle. In the meantime, "protecting" women against combat training is merely a pretext for refusing them the higher pay scales which go with combat duty. Male egoism thus not only inflicts injustice on those women who might become first-rate fighters. It also keeps the quality of the fighting forces lower (at the same cost) or keeps them more expensive (for the same quality of forces) than would happen without this form of discrimination. The pattern of social waste is familiar. Its application to the military forces is all the more appalling when we are talking about forces which are supposed to guarantee the survival of the nation and its freedoms.

LEADERSHIP AND MANAGERIAL COMPETENCE

Managerial competence is one variety or facet of technical competence which only recently has come to full attention. When the classical economists, from Adam Smith to Marx and on down to Marshall, specified the factors of production, they only mentioned "land, labor and capital". They did not mention management; at best it was thought of as a special case of labor. This may be because in those days managerial talent was surplus hence not a scarce good, and economists deal only in scarce goods. The practical failures of applied Marxism flow to a large extent from this oversight. It would of course have confounded their mechanistic schemes if they had to account for something as personal as managerial ability. Absence of incentives to managerial initiatives has become a blight which weighs down progress in the Soviet economy and makes them rely on imports (bought or stolen) of inventions made in the "capitalist" world. In the extreme case, they even purchased a whole managerial model as in the Italian designed automobile factory in "Togliattigrad". The essence is capitalist, only the name Communist.

The modern scene is strikingly different from the talent surplus of the age of early classical economics. Managerial talent at all levels is now at a premium and generally well paid. Too well, sometimes: for access to the ranks of management is hampered by discrimination against women and minority men, as well as by the strictures of "positional goods", of which more below. As if there were not enough proof in other sectors of the economy, we need only point to the school system as a case in point, for here the ranks are largely women, yet the leadership (the school principals) are mainly men. Discrimination in management and leadership positions is to the short-run advantage of those benefiting by it.

Usually these men do not comprehend that this kind of privilege makes society poorer than it might be, and that this also makes them—often mediocre white men—collectively poorer than they might be in a more freely competitive society. Many of them are too mediocre to think that far. Avoiding the trap of the "Peter principle" (being promoted beyond the range of one's real competence) takes brains as well as character.

In regard to positions of leadership and social prominence, discrimination is particularly destructive for an additional reason. Even as the labor market cries out for more high-competent people in the ranks and intermediate levels it has, in fact, fewer openings for the kinds of positions where the individual stands out from the crowd. "Positional goods" (Fred Hirsch), those offering the advantage of being in the public eye with all that this brings with it of power and money, these advanced positions are relatively fewer than ever before. One reason is that the population continues to increase. Another is in the increasingly hierarchical structure of big business and public administration. There can only be one President of the United States at any one time, only 100 Senators, and so on. The larger the population, the smaller the statistical chance for any one individual of reaching any of these numerically rationed positions. In many walks of life it is even worse because of increasing centralization. In the arts and public entertainment, the "star effect" of being on a widely watched stage, screen, or publisher's list, is more rare now than in the age of the "show boat" and the family-owned newspaper or publishing house. The bureaucratization of the world, both East and West (Henry Jacoby) also leads to fewer, not more, places of prominence to compete for. Industrial mergers and cartel formations similarly render ever fewer those individuals who can stand on the commanding heights of society and steer its direction. So much the more dangerous then is any tendency to shut out some kinds of people from the paths that lead on high, and so much the more essential is it that talent is recruited from the broadest possible base so that leadership can reach the highest level of quality that society can engender, as well as become representative of all its intrinsic variety.

VARIETY OF TALENT

"Variety is the spice of life", a principle all too evident in all kinds of public entertainment, from vaudeville artists to politicians. It is far from being limited to them but it is easiest to start there because entertainment in all its forms belongs to our common everyday experience.

The prevalence of white men in American media was striking until quite recently—so recently that women and minority persons as yet have only rarely advanced to senior positions. Ironically, the Soviet radio knew better long ago. Already in the time of Stalin, Radio Moscow had a male and a female voice alternating in reading the news, thus to some extent easing up the monotonous droning of their performance. But in small-town America, it was thought all right to have two white men—resembling each other as Tweedledum and Tweedledee—alternating in a performance which could not have been duller by one of them doing it alone. Like a disturbed sleepwalker, the station "woke up and smelled the coffee" only when the women's movement had been knocking at their doors for some time.

This tendency toward caste monopoly in American media is all the more surprising as male monopoly had already been broken in other kinds of entertainment for the sheer reason of variety. It is long since we ceased to have female roles on the stage played by masquerading men (in the Orient, this continued much longer). The movies never had this role reversal in America, and in fiction writing it has been some time since women writers tried to conceal their identities behind male-sounding pseudonyms. Black artists first gained prominence because of a particular quality in music, and it took some time to realize that black actors and writers belong in America's cultural scene for the simple reason that black people belong among the population of the country.

The principle of variety is far from mysterious. Technical competence must be complemented by human competence, both for leadership roles and for the many situations where human qualities affect the outcome of economic and other practical endeavor.

For instance, in the United Nations and its specialized agencies, where I worked over a stretch of years, professional personnel is recruited (at considerable cost) under an elaborate system of nationality quotas—the details can be omitted here. This was not just intended to unruffle the feathers of newly indpendent poor countries who were jealous about their status and who also wanted some listening ears of their own inside the organizations. It was also generally understood and widely accepted that organizations dealing with the affairs of the whole world could not be run competently by Americans and Europeans only, no matter how superior such cadres might be in conventional technical terms. Being from Africa, or India, or South America, for instance, is also a special kind of competence—the competence of intimate knowledge of the home country or region, at both the factual and the emotional levels. This competence is indispensable for the interaction of nations.

The same should have been self evident in the relations of this country with other countries, but strangely enough it is far from always observed. The original "ugly American" (Lederer and Burdick)—a widely misunderstood term—had grasped this, but most of the "beautiful people" in U.S. embassies and military missions had not. We should by now have learned the penalty for this kind of incompetence.

But we have the same need for variety of human competence within the United States. This country can not be identified with any one culture, creed, or other grouping except the nation itself. Old-world nations with ingrained traditions of petty empire may still feel more secure when ruled by an elite which is clearly identified as to language, accent, culture, religion (or, pseudo-religion) or whatever. But none of this applies to the "Land of the Free". This "melting-pot" country is in many ways the precursor of a world community to come. We have no "King's English", nor "Queen's English" for that matter. Even the WASPs are a minority in their own country and in most if not all of the states. A recent essay on the "nine nations of America" (Joel Garreau) shows some of the cleavages within this country. There are certainly many others that could be cited. Any one group that might succeed in cornering some important function in America would make the country smaller by reducing its invigorating polycentrism. So would any reactionary policy which identifies the United States with some only among its past traditions and experiences rather than with its present needs and future prospects.

To return to the politicians, they too have something in common with entertainers, witness the success of some former entertainers in politics. One who knew this and lived by it was the late Everett Dirksen, Republican Senator from Illinois. His "Ev and Charlie Show" on a television (with Charles Halleck, or "Available Charlie", a Republican congressman from Ohio) consciously sought to capitalize on politics as "the best show in town"; only, the two white gentlemen brought rather little variety to their broadcast endeavor. Even as entertainment, politics would give the public better value by having more women and minority men on the cast.

But politics is of course also serious business; at least the consequences for us are serious. And this would undoubtedly be better served by including among the politicians more of the same variety as there is in the population. For instance, being a woman also implies a special kind of competence, one which men do not have. A woman's place is really both in the House and the Senate. Only if they are there in force can the legislative bodies become representative of the sovereign people and consider all its needs and aspirations, economic and otherwise.

The same applies to all the professions where there is a need for a human touch. The police, for instance, was long thought of as a men's preserve because of the greater body strength of the average man. Recent experience with female police officers has proven something quite different. Not only are women officers better at handling female offenders; they often impress male criminals with more respect too. Firearms are of course neutral to both gender and body strength, and so are the martial arts which we have learned from eastern Asia. In addition, we are told, female officers are better at the psychological handling of the human wrecks they have to steer through police procedures. Police work, it now appears, is more than shootouts and physical overpowering. It has sufficiently much to do with human relations so that a mixed police force is more efficient, hence also more cost effective, than a purely male one—or, a purely white one, for that matter.

The lesson seems hard to drive home in other traditional male preserves such as the medical professions. To take a crude example, the much publicized Mr. Bakke, whatever his conventional abilities, is because of his attitude intrinsically unfit to practice medicine among black patients. If he had been fit for that, he would also have understood the nature of the problem and would then never have attempted his "reverse discrimination" suit. "Affirmative action" is more than just a belated attempt (and as yet a rather clumsy one) at doing justice toward individuals and groups which have been wronged in the past. More than that, it should also aim at doing justice toward society, the nation, and the world. Not merely because without it we can not look the world in the eye and speak of human rights, but also because without it we will be economically weaker and less fit to bear the standard of freedom in the world either in peaceful ventures or in war, if it should come to that.

COMPETITIVE JUSTICE

Competition, the invigorating influence of having a chance and of having to face other people's chances, has always been hailed as one of the national hallmarks of the United States. Why is it then so hard to admit its full impact and consequence? Not only does free competition admit all who have the talent, the training and the drive to compete for jobs and advancement. It also injects some of the drive and motivates some of that training effort into the ranks of those who otherwise become discouraged workers, a large component in today's unemployment.

The human damage from discouragement is not limited to the discouraged individuals, be they inner-city black youths perceiving no horizon, or claustrophobic housewives trapped in a web spun around them by destructive mythical forces such as the "feminine mystique" (Betty Friedan). Just as much, the discouragement caused by discrimination or other forces that limit competition lowers work morale and productivity, both of those unjustly excluded from competition and of those unjustly favored. The parallel lowering of civic morale, and of the moral stance toward the defense of the country, are indirectly harmful to the economy as well.

This extends also to "social origin" as a cause of less than unhampered competition. This factor can not be discounted even in America. The poor will always be with us. Any cursory reading of income statistics shows that there are inequalities of income everywhere in the world. This is so also in Communist countries where the ideology has been modified recently to say that complete equality serves no purpose. As a practical matter, incomes in those countries have tended to become more and more unequal, as the fruits of incipient affluence are trickling up more than down, by means which are often technically illegal in communist societies.

Looking merely at the free world, the degrees of inequality are very different, even within a large country such as the United

States. The upper Midwest has about as much equality as Scandinavia, while the Deep South is half-way to approaching the extreme inequalities of Latin America. The point to be made has to do with opportunities for economic advancement, hence also the efficiency of society's access to its talent pool. The narrow income distributions, as in the upper Midwest and in Scandinavia, mean that most people are born, and live, in middle-class conditions. The poor are then a minority and their chance of advancing, individually, into middle-class conditions are fairly good, statistically speaking. The positions to which these upward mobile people may aspire are much more numerous than the upward mobile individuals themselves. Under extreme inequality, as in Latin America and (to a less extreme degree) some sections of the American South, the poor are, by contrast, a large part of the population. Therefore, many of them can just as well give up hope of ever getting anywhere in life. The potential openings are fewer than the potential aspirants for upward mobility, and they are also more jealously guarded by those fortunate enough already to be in those favored positions. Thus, with sharper economic class divisions, both upward and downward mobility is hampered, and society does not get the full benefit of its total talent pool. Severe income inequality compounds the effects of discrimination by sex and "race" and becomes partially merged with these: women and minority men are poor more often than are men of the favored category.

PENALTIES FOR DISCRIMINATION

Some of this had been mentioned above, case by case. The damage done by discrimination is of course easiest to discern in extreme cases. The author of "The Godfather" (Mario Puso) poses the problem squarely in his section from Sicily: because the criminal Organization placed loyalty to itself above all else, they eliminated—for instance—a first-rate physician who had become inconvenient because of his honesty. Thus they had to be served by a low-competent quack instead. And so it went, with Organization loyalty corroding all levels of society in and around itself. In this way, the Organization generated real poverty indirectly even more than it did by its direct stealing.

The counterparts of criminal Organization loyalty are not hard to find if we look in the right places. One frequent case is nepotism, as for instance when a utility company has to accept as foreman an individual whose main merit is being a relative of an influential politician. Discrimination in favor of white men is in fact the same thing on a systematic scale and the penalty for nepotism is, as always, mediocrity.

The same goes not only for discrimination by sex and "race". It extends also to "social origin". The meaning of this for the recruiting of talent was touched upon above. Extreme inequality leads to greater difficulty in finding and training high talent. Maintaining more inequality in society than is needed as incentive for advancement is therefore also a form of discrimination which is harmful to the economy by engendering social waste—the waste of potential talent.

Along with this we have the general problem of widespread poverty, and the social programs intended to alleviate it. Widespread poverty hurts society by lowering the quality of its labor force and its incentives, that much we should already be able to agree upon. A second point, which many "conservatives" miss is their perception of social programs as "charity", something we may elect to do out of the goodness of our hearts but could also elect not to do if we find other matters to be of greater interest. This overlooks the role of social programs for maintaining peace in the community.

It is an age-old experience that if the poor become very numerous and are left without any help, they will band together for robbery. Even traditional penury societies have usually understood this. An example is Mediaeval Iceland which already had a statute for the economic care of the poor—a "safety net". It was not a very generous arrangement, that would not have been possible at the time, but the basic guarantee was there. Abandoning the poor to their own lot—that is, to robbery—is not only a solution which makes us lose some of our humanity; it would also be quite costly in terms of policing. In many poor countries, the problem takes the form of protection rackets—ostensibly large numbers of paid retainers but in reality so many potential robbers who would take by force the elemental livelihood which society, and its rich people, might endeavor to withhold from them in the name of "sanctity of property". In a bread riot, there is nothing sacred about property; life is more sacred, and the command to preserve life was laid down in our nature long before there was any private property system.

Those who dislike social programs because they mean taxing of private wealth would do well, therefore, to consider the fact that the existence and the security of property depend upon the legal order in society being free from serious disturbances. And that such freedom from internal strife can not be guaranteed in face of widespread poverty without relief. Maintaining a safety net is more than charity—it is a necessity to maintain civilized society.

RUNNING JUST TO STAY IN PLACE?

Much of what has been said above about discrimination in America is relative. The country has made some progress of late. Much of that progress looks larger from a distance than it does on close inspection. The question is not, have women and the minorities, and the socially disadvantaged, made any progress? Rather, the question should be, has there been as much of it as the economic situation would have called for?

The answer is no—not by a long shot. Looking at the wage differences (the women's 59 cents which appear rather constant), it is evident that women's talents are not being drawn into highly qualified positions to anywhere near the extent the economy would need. Alice in Wonderland comes to mind: when you are running on a carpet that rolls away from under you, you have to run very fast just to stay in place.

This is too bad, and not just because there still are strong retarding forces of inertia and shortsighted group egoism to make the pace of progress slower than it might be. Worse still, the political climate in the early 1980's has favored retrogression. Political leaders in charge have evidently not begun to understand the changes in economy and society under way in the past half century. When their favoring of the unjustly favored is cloaked in slogans about traditional values and the national interest, some serious misunderstandings are under foot. Predicting the past, and calling it the future, is based on nothing better than wishful thinking which is the stuff disasters are made of.

Ironically, such conservative thinking is also contrary to the needs of national defense, which will require that we mobilize all the resources we have.

Chapter 9
Defense Sinkhole

The defense establishment is a large and costly sector of the American economy. In themselves, defense expenditures are not social waste, not if we look at the world as it is today and recognize the need for defense now and in the foreseeable future. But more than any of the civilian sectors, defense needs watching for waste, obsolescence and redundancy, for here we have a perfectly socialist sector. No market forces can correct what the defense establishment does wrong so as to provoke social waste. Private enterprise in warfare is a minor nuisance on the international scene, mainly among small countries which have not yet completed their nation building. A large polity such as the United States can not tolerate private armies; all armed might of any consequence has to be the monopoly of the national government. In the Occident, this has been so ever since the Viking fleets were socialized by Canute the Great (died A.D. 1035). Nor can defense be farmed out to a parapublic corporation such as the Postal Service; much less can it be contracted to a utility company such as AT&T.

As a completely socialized sector, defense in the United States has the capacity to devour resources without any even approximate check on the rationality of what it is doing. Redundancy and duplication are continuous problems; so are cost over-runs. At the same time, some of the concomitant advantages such as the stabilizing influence of a command sector (a sector which spends in good times and bad, without regard to business cycles), and the technological spinoffs generated by defense oriented research, are not unique to defense; they can be obtained also from civilian oriented command sectors and related research and development.

The sky is not the limit for defense expenditures; the capacity of the economy is. Long before any absolute limit is approached, we have to watch for the risks that the civilian economy may be impaired by avoidable defense expenditures. Such damage to the civilian economy would in the end impair also the country's defense posture, both for material reasons and because of morale-problems. And, to turn the problem inside out, if unavoidable defense needs turn out to be heavy, how could the civilian sectors make up for this, if not by cutting out some of the social waste by which they are now riddled?

DEFENSE AS AN ECONOMIC SINKHOLE

Defense is a consumer. Like the civilian economy, it absorbs large quantities of nearly all the kinds of goods and services which the economy turns out, from food, clothing and shelter, to heavy hardware and educational facilities. Defense shares all the "backward linkages" of the economy—the lines of supply from raw materials to factory production through the distribution system—and hence, defense expenditures have the same kind of stimulating effect on the various sectors which supply the defense requirements, as has civilian demand for goods and services intended both for consumption and investment. Unlike the civilian economy, however, the defense establishment does not ordinarily generate any new production. Exceptions are in the education of military personnel which often renders them more productive also in the civilian economy to which many of them transfer after their military contracts are terminated. Defense related research and development also generate some innovations of value to the economy as a whole, of which more below.

But on the whole, there are no "forward linkages" from the defense sector to new production in industry or other civilian sectors. Heavy hardware, fuel, and highly competent manpower are in the civilian economy used not only for consumption, as in housing, transportation, and other "consumer durables", but also in productive investment such as for the construction and equipping of new factories etc., and for upgrading or maintaining of old ones. Investment is what makes the civilian economy grow (become larger) and develop (become more productive). The military, by contrast, does not invest in factories or in transportation for production purposes. It also uses heavy hardware, often with highly complex engineering designs embodying the fruits of the labor of highly competent manpower. But the defense establishment invests these expensive goods in weapons systems, and these do not contribute to national product. They just sit there, in readiness and for training purposes, generating protection against the nation's potential enemies both foreign and domestic. Saying that weapons systems are not economically productive is not a very startling statement, but it needs to be emphasized as the very basis for all else we may have to say about the economics of defense. Because it is almost entirely consumptive and contributes little to economic production, the defense system adds to the scarcity of investment means. This scarcity is at the root of recent and current problems of slow economic growth in the United States. These problems, in their turn, render more difficult to supply the defense system with all that it needs.

Recent history has given us some striking lessons on this connection between defense needs and investment in the economy. The two main losers in World War II were Germany and Japan. Both took the world by surprise by their "economic miracles", the unexpected and unparalleled speed with which they repaired their severely war-damaged economies and launched into a period of prosperity such as neither had ever seen before. What many people failed to notice is that these economic miracles took place while both countries were legally prohibited from having any defense establishment at all. Now they share some of it, and their economic growth rates have slowed down.

The victors, by contrast, were visibly hampered by their continuing defense burden. This has been particularly evident in the United Kingdom which came out of the war as the only important military power in Europe outside the Soviet Union. The U.K. has carried the burden with difficulty and has experienced slow and uneven economic growth. The United States has shouldered most of the burden of defense of the free world, including two major wars far away from this country. This country has also suffered from economic growth rates which have been slower than those in much of the free world. Private American investment abroad is not the only explanation for this. American defense costs have also contributed. More recently, the Soviet Union has also begun to show the strain of a large burden of armaments build-up. The massive expansion of warships and heavy weapons systems under Brezhnev has contributed to slowing down the economic growth rate of that country far below what it was in earlier periods. In recent years, Soviet economic growth has been a good deal slower than that of the world as a whole. They never had any world record of rapid economic growth to begin with—they never matched the long-term rates of Japan or Mexico, for instance.

Military-economic thinkers in this country have even suggested, recently, that the United States, by continuing the arms race, could break the back of the Soviet economy. If such a policy were under way to attaining its objective, the consequences for the world scene might be rather unpredictable. But the logic limps: if armaments could ruin their economy, so it could ruin ours.

THE SINKHOLE DEEPENS

Defense is getting heavier to bear, more expensive in real terms. This is because of the increasing scarcity of capital, a change which ultimately derives from the energy problem, as set out in Chapter 3 above. It is therefore misleading to count, as some people do, only the percentage of the national product that goes into defense, and specifically into material supplies for defense. This percentage is not much different now from what it has been in recent decades, but in making such comparisons we must look also at the composition of the economy, of the capital markets, and of defense investment. How the defense investment relates to the whole question of investible resources in the economy is critical for the effects which defense expenditures may have on the economy as a whole.

The pool of savings generated by the American economy is rather shallow. The ways in which savings are distributed between productive investment and investment serving only consumption is therefore critical to the ability of the economy to grow and develop. Energy costs weigh heavier than before on both consumption and investment, and not just because of the higher real prices at which energy goods (such as fuels and electric power) are traded. Equally important are two other things: the energy sector itself is getting more energy intensive, more capital intensive and more expertise intensive. And civilian consumption also tends to become more energy intensive and capital intensive by the larger shares of transportation (mainly by automobiles) and housing—in consumption or in the economy as a whole. In this double pinch, from energy costs and from rising energy use in civilian consumption, the capital markets tend to become more strained, as we should learn from recent history on interest rates. Therefore, the same amounts or percentages of defense expenditures for "commodities" (read: weapons systems) now weigh heavier on the economy. The same rate of defense spending no longer has the same meaning as before.

In short, defense expenditures are heavier than before because they tend to drain the same sectors of the civilian economy which have been hit the hardest by the consequences of the energy problem. We must earnestly question whether the country can carry both the defense burdens now being proposed and in part already implemented, and the continuation of social waste as it exists, and particularly in the energy sector—specifically in energy intensive consumption sectors such as automobiles and housing. But we must not overlook waste in the military sector itself.

COST OVERRUNS, OBSOLESCENCE AND REDUNDANCY

The most persistent complaint about military procurements is about cost overruns. Contracts are let, usually after competitive bidding, and when the bills come due they are often much larger than was contracted for. Excuses are often found in inflation and in various causes of rising real costs. Among these is now the cost of capital under a regimen of high real interest rates. The enlarged bills are honored so routinely that only delays in many deliveries rescue the Department of Defense budget from being blown completely to pieces.

Politicians are understandably irritated at these endless cost overruns, but there is little that can be done about this problem. Refusing payment could bankrupt some companies which might jeopardize continued weapons deliveries. Besides, no politician wants to throw people out of work, least of all those in high-wage industries such as those manufacturing military hardware.

There may be a problem of how cost estimates are made, and of how they are approved in the negotiations between the DoD and the manufacturers. Maybe the industries routinely understate the costs they anticipate, as a means of securing the contracts—safe as they are in the expectation that their bills will be honored, cost overruns and all. Contracting with a command sector which has no competition is like no other contracting in the world.

One conclusion is that we must form our opinions about the cost of defense from past budgets. The forward budgets we are presented with by the government and those eventually approved by Congress, are less than completely conclusive as to what the defense will cost when the bills are in. No matter how the problem is turned around, it makes even more urgent the search for the most economical set of weapons systems that can be found.

Obsolescence is one problem. It was noted in debates recently in connection with the program of refurbishing old battle ships from World War II. Are these more than floating targets, sitting ducks for today's heat seeking missiles and other super weapons? From the Spanish Armada (1588) to the Battle of Tsushima Straits (1905) and on to the sinking of battleships such as the Hood and the Bismarck in World War II, we should have learned that large surface ships need to be on the level of the most recent technology to be of any military value. The Falklands battle gave some ominous lessons on how vulnerable large surface ships can be for attacks by much cheaper units such as planes with air-to-surface missiles.

The problem of obsolescence is of course equally important in assessing the strength of a potential enemy. Soviet tanks and planes should not only be counted for their numbers but also weighed as to their operational adequacy. Efficiency of fire power is more essential than its size.

Between cost overruns and possible obsolescence we have the more general problem of duplication and redundancy. This is a large economic problem in its consequences, but most of the arguments are technical and have to be settled by military and engineering expertise. In recent debate, we have heard military experts, such as General Maxwell Taylor, define "task readiness" and conclude that it can be achieved at much less cost than was proposed in recent budget requests from the DoD. The extreme case of duplication is of course in the tradeoff between nuclear weapons and conventional ones, and here the arguments are not only those put forward by the experts.

NUCLEAR OVERKILL

The "nuclear umbrella", we are told, is the ultimate defense against Soviet aggression in Europe. It functioned that way in the 1950's when the nuclear arsenals were much smaller than now. So, why could it not still work the same way—the more the better?

The enormous size of the nuclear arsenals is in fact the main problem. Against nuclear weapons there is no defense. There is only the deterrent of the threat of a counterattack with nuclear weapons which would be too devastating for any enemy to sustain. Because of the present size of the nuclear arsenals on both sides of a potential conflict, all-out nuclear war would mean planetary suicide. Secondary effects such as damage to the ozone layer in the upper atmosphere, or the "nuclear winter", would extinguish all life except small species. People, as well as their food base, would vanish.

What purpose do these over-sized nuclear arsenals serve, then? None at all, that is the answer. A deterrent so large that it eventually annihilates also the power which uses it has simply left the domain of rational reasoning. It can only be explained as a continuation of military routine thinking on conventional weapons. Machine guns firing a million rounds to kill ten enemy soldiers, artillery barrages directed at enemy positions just to keep the enemy down in his trenches while one's own troops advance closer to their positions, "saturation bombardment", and so on, these are applications of conventional fire power which have been found economical because they substitute material for manpower. Obviously, such uses of non-nuclear explosives have no counterpart in nuclear weapons. Only a fraction of the nuclear arms we now have could be used without causing irreparable damage to the earth's ecology.

The question is then raised as to why do we not seek a gradual, mutual reduction in nuclear weapons and replace them by building up conventional armed forces until we have enough of those to meet any threat to the free world by conventional weapons? The typical military answer is that nuclear weapons are more cost effective. So they are indeed, and that is just the core of the problem. Nuclear explosives are by far and away the most cost effective means ever invented to kill large numbers of people, destroy whole cities, and so on. The cost of doing the same damage by TNT would be many times higher. But what good is the cost effectiveness of nuclear weapons when they can not, rationally speaking, be used? To contemplate their use in "limited" nuclear war, their numbers must first be reduced to the point that the use could be limited. As long as we have these present large arsenals, we can trust the military on the losing side to fire away all they have, regardless of the ultimate danger to their own country.

Even "limited" nuclear war would be likely to cause us more damage than we can survive as a nation. Long before the ecosphere of the earth is seriously threatened, the economy and polity would be torn to shreds. Loss of fuel would be one reason. One-tenth of the Soviet nuclear arsenal would be sufficient to wipe out all our oil refinery capacity, and unlike destruction by conventional explosives, the bombarded sites could not be entered upon for repairs for a long time to come. The food chain and other vital supplies would also be disrupted beyond any repair within the span of time that would be indispensable—all remedies would come too late. The U.S. economy is extremely dependent on transportation, courtesy the automobile and truck systems which were developed on the assumption—among other optimistic assumptions—that peace on this continent would be guaranteed forever. All the official plans for survival after a limited nuclear attack are just so much paper exercise serving no purpose but to mislead the public.

The conclusion is that in one way or another the nuclear arsenals must be reduced. They must be reduced to whatever level is still needed as an ultimate deterrent against reckless war gambles by big powers or small ones. It is inevitable that the burden of conventional defense expenditures will be heavier in this way. This only places even more emphasis on the twin premises of this chapter: that defense must become as economical as it possibly can be made, and that we can not afford the social waste which is rampant in the civilian economy, especially in transportation and housing.

ECONOMIC STABILIZER

The place of defense in our national economy includes a paradox: this truly socialist sector is cherished the most by the same people—"conservatives"—who generally abhor socialism in any form, shape, or guise. Only when leaving office did President Eisenhower articulate his warning against the "military-industrial complex" as a threat to the American economy.

At the other end of the political spectrum there are many who deplore a large defense burden because of the sinkhole that it is, and because it competes with civilian purposes such as those of social insurance, health care, and a better level of living for people in general and for low-income people in particular.

Only seldom do we hear, either from the left or the right, of defense as an economic stabilizer. Back in the "roaring twenties", when the public sectors (both defense and civilian) were small, the U.S. economy eventually stumbled into the Great Depression, beginning with the stock market crash in the fall of 1929. That Depression became deeper and lasted longer than previous "panics" of the 1800's, because the income level was higher than ever before and because, in the absence of high taxation or large public sectors, people's "discretionary income" (the part of the income they can do with as they please) was a larger part than ever of the whole national economy. Among the things you can do with discretionary income is refuse to spend it when the economic outlook is troublesome. Hence there was nothing to stop the depression from feeding on itself, in a continuous downward spiral. Even the first attempts at counter cyclical policy (public deficit spending during economic downturns, and vice versa) had difficulty coming to grips with this downward tendency all at once.

There are several reasons why this kind of deep and lasting depression has not happened again, after the 1930's. Among these reasons is the lesson learned, and the now more refined techniques of counter cyclical economic policy. Other reasons are in the now large economic stabilizers. These include the public sectors, foremost among them defense and social insurance, which now claim a much larger share of the national product than in the 1920's. The public sectors go forward and spend in bad times and good. The stabilizers also include the quasi necessities created by the institutionalizing of certain private spending habits, especially those of transportation and housing which have their levels in part guaranteed by "multiple lock-in" systems bolstered by tax policies. Thus, discretionary income is now in reality not as large a share of the national product as it was before the Great Depression.

This blessing in disguise from large public expenditures seems to be well disguised on the whole. Not only is it hidden from view for a large part of the public but also for many responsible politicians. Only when it comes to specific contracts such as deliveries of military airplanes from such and such factory, are the politicians alive to the pork-barrel aspect of this. Much is then made of the employment effect, without regard for the employment foregone by not spending the same amounts in some other sector of the economy.

As stabilizers go, however, defense expenditures have no particular advantage over those in the civilian sectors. The employment effect is often lower in defense hardware because it costs much capital and expertise and not so much ordinary labor. Thus the money set in circulation by defense expenditures tends to go, in the first place, to people in the upper income strata. Social insurance, on the other hand, does as much good as defense expenditures to stabilize the economy, but it does not use up as much capital as does the defense budget. The employment effect of social expenditures is likely to be greater because more of the pensions and unemployment insurance payments go to pay for basic consumer goods. Thus, we do not have to keep a high level of defense expenditures merely to support a faltering economy.

TECHNOLOGICAL SPINOFFS

As a command economy, defense sets off some economic consequences which might not be prompted with as much vigor by market forces. The case is well known from the subsidizing of manufactures in older European history (1600's, 1700's): subsidized and tariff protected factories making, for instance, clothing or shoes might turn out substandard goods, and they could go on doing this for quite some time. But those making rifles or cannons were not tolerated to be inefficient: either the guns could shoot or they could not. War (or the prospect of it) is more coercive than peacetime consumer demand.

This was in relatively primitive industrial beginnings. A parallel tendency has been observed in the Soviet economy until quite recently: consumer goods industries were systematically given low-quality inputs to work with, and in their output low quality was tolerated up to a surprisingly high degree of shoddiness. But the military sector in the USSR has also, systematically, been given the best of what the economy could turn out, and so their military hardwares are closer to what they are supposed to be; which does not necessarily mean that they are all that they are supposed to be.

There are many cases in recent military and industrial history where military needs have accelerated inventions and innovations which would eventually benefit the civilian economy. Aviation is a stock example: World War I turned the fledgling airplane into a viable form of alternative transportation in both war and peace. More recently, military requirements and plans have prompted nuclear-generated electric power. As an option to produce large parts of the energy needs of the future, nuclear power still has many question marks attached to it. In this case, there was a political desire to justify nuclear weapons by showing a spinoff which would be useful to civilian consumption. Thus a new industry was built up for the wrong reason. Eventually, space research also led to applications of rocket technology—initially a weapons program—in ways which are in part of benefit to civilian purposes.

The supremacy of military over civilian purposes is a primitive trait, however. *A priori* there is no reason why inventions made for reasons of civilian consumption should not also prove useful in war. The early case in point is gunpowder which was invented in China to be used in fireworks, then turned into artillery explosive by the Mongol conquerors. In modern time we know better than before what we are doing in scientific research and technological development. Command research can be done with equal effect from a civilian as from a military starting point. The decisive thing is that we support long-range research and development, not only the type for immediate purpose. Much of the long-range R&D is in fact financed by the public powers, in this country foremost by the Federal government.

Technological spinoffs are thus not a merit specific to military technology. We should not tolerate defense expenditures which are larger than needed just because of expected technological spinoffs.

STABILITY, SUPERIORITY, AND SMALL GANGSTERS

How large the military budget needs to be depends also on the scope of the military-political objectives which are to be secured by the existence (if not always the actual use) of military forces. "Task readiness" must be understood in relation to the tasks that may have to be performed or at least credibly suggested to a potential adversary. President Nixon's statement that this nation can not be "the policeman of the world" appears to have been reversed, at least in part, by his successors. The "rapid deployment force" was designed for quick responses far away.

When it comes to superpower relations, we have a real problem of superiority versus stability. Will "the other side" become more reasonable by feeling inferior or by feeling secure? We can not have it both ways. Superpower politics is a balancing act, best characterized by Dean Acheson's policy of "containment". Trying to be or to become decisively superior, we must expect war as the response early on our path toward superiority. Not keeping up approximate equality we risk very much the same.

Beyond the superpower relations and how far they can be harnessed to a lower level of total armaments (and especially those of the nuclear variety), there is more and more the problem of small gangsters on the international scene. Idi Amin of Uganda had his designs on neighboring countries. Mu'ammar Qaddafi of Libya is still at it. The Argentine generals, not content with a domestic war of extermination against political adversaries, had to launch their country into an international adventure because they underestimated the resolve of Britain. War between Iran and Iraq can only be described as two madmen fighting in a dark room not knowing what they are doing. There would no doubt be more reckless small-power adventures were it not for the readiness of the large powers to intervene when small conflicts threaten to get out of hand. The petty empire building of Viet Nam in Cambodia and Laos should tell us something.

NO END IN SIGHT

The sketch just drawn of a need for military-political stabilizers leaves little reason to hope for relief from military requirements any time soon. There are however at least two things which domestic economic policy might contribute to render the military burden more bearable and more compatible with objectives of economic growth and development and of continued social progress.

One has already been alluded to: the de-emphasizing of energy intensive and capital intensive consumption sectors of the civilian economy, such as transportation and housing, will free up resources both for productive civilian investments (including those of defense related industries) and for direct military procurements, with less of a conflict to be resolved between these sectors.

The other concerns imported oil. Part of the rationale for a large defense burden (and particularly the rapid deployment force) is in the perceived need to defend our vital interests far away, such as in the Persian Gulf area. With less individual transportation, hence less use of liquid fuel, the United State might disengage from its dependence on foreign energy sources, and this might render the tasks for defense somehat less overwhelming. The Persian Gulf area might not be as vital to us as it appears now. To live in peace with the world, one essential contribution would be that this continental nation comes closer to living within its own means as regards basic natural resources.

Chapter 10
The Conditions for Unlimited Economic Growth

Economic growth is a value as cherished as apple pie. But unlike the apple pie, few people can tell what economic growth is. What does it mean, really? The theme of this book is social waste, and before summing up the conclusions of the preceding chapters we must take a close look at the meaning of economic growth. How much of it is wasted, how much really adds to human satisfaction? And how long can it go on?

The problem was placed in sharper focus for us a dozen years ago when limits to growth were spelled out by a group known as the Club of Rome. The energy problem should rub in the same lesson: due to the unprecedented quantity development of the modern world economy, we are forced to acknowledge that the earth is finite. In a dramatic formulation, our planet has been likened to a space ship—"Spaceship Earth" (Buckminster Fuller). A ship is a closed universe which must live by rather stringent discipline to remain viable.

If the drain on the earth's material resources goes on unabated, with the same growth rates as in the recent past, these material resources will all be exhausted in less than a century—so the Club of Rome concluded. It would not even help much if the resources were to turn out to be three times as large as they are conventionally assumed to be: with the growth rates of the past, snowballing by the compound-interest principle, the funds of energy and scarce minerals would then last only twenty years longer than under the "base case" of conventionally accepted resource estimates.

This limit to physical resources is in one sense a trivial fact. Yet the limit to growth, as stated by the Club of Rome, is a simplification set forth for the sake of argument. If it were taken literally, it would be a half truth, but it would not be a total fallacy either. There are really conditions under which economic growth may be viewed as virtually limitless, but these conditions are by no means as easy as they are sometimes made to appear by purveyors of false good news. Above all, they are not compatible with large-scale social waste, nor with unlimited population growth into the remote future.

The conditions for unlimited economic growth are partly conceptual and partly material. Some conceptual or definitional issues must be clarified so that we can agree on what economic growth is. Some material conditions must also be fulfilled: in regard to the mix of factors in production, the mix of goods in consumption, and the use of technological substitution to modify both of these mixes.

MEANING OF ECONOMIC GROWTH

We are talking about the expansion of national product: the systems of production and consumption grow larger. National product accounts can be criticized in many ways—it is always easier to criticize than to propose a better system. After all, we have had systematic national accounting only since around 1930. What we know (or, think that we know) about national product in older times has been reconstructed for us by research in economic history. Recently there have even been proposals to revise the concept of national product, through the National Bureau of Economic Research (J. W. Kendrick). There have also been efforts to re-measure national product in many countries by using international prices as a common yardstick, so as to make the accounts more comparable between countries (by I. Kravis and associates, for the World Bank). Both of these recent research endeavors point to the enormous difficulties we have in rendering the concept of national product and its growth clear even to experts, let alone then to the public in general.

For our present purpose we must focus on certain conceptual difficulties which could easily lead us astray. These include bulk versus value, overhead disutility, hidden productivity gains, the problem of cost of production versus value in use, and the nature of current and future advances in production.

VALUE AND VOLUME

Value product, that is production of economic value or production worth having, does not have to have always the same amounts of physical material in it, which is what the Club of Rome calculations assumed at least implicitly. National product is measured by value, not by bulk or weight. Otherwise a brick factory would be more impressive than a plant making precision instruments. Thus the definition of economic growth also does not necessitate any increase in the use of raw materials. In many lines of production, smaller items are in fact more valuable than larger ones. A wristwatch is more useful than a grandfather clock, at least to those of us who are not aficionados of old clocks. A switch in the composition of output toward higher-value articles can produce economic growth even though mining and other extractive industries were held constant or even contracted.

PRODUCTION AND ENVIRONMENT

Next, we must understand conflicts such as those of production versus environmental quality. When increased production of material goods fouls up the air and the waters, cramps the traffic system and deteriorates human relations, then production has generated *disutilities* along with the utility of the goods produced. Such disutility generally escapes conventional accounting because it is a social overhead, it is not contracted or traded between parties on a market. It also tends to be more difficult to measure than production of goods, and it often falls on people in different proportions than their share in the consumption and enjoyment of the goods. The rich are often in a position to live—as on mansions and ranches—far away from the stink, the chemical dangers and other physical hazards, and the human degradation caused by the production of what they enjoy. The poor are likely to get more than their share of the inconveniences that come from the things someone else enjoys.

Disutilities are to some extent re-introduced into the national accounts by the cost of measures such as those for pollution abatement or more complete re-cycling of waste materials even when low profitable. Production of goods to serve pollution abatement, for instance, begins to be a sizeable component of manufacturing industry, which is why the business press (such as the *Wall Street Journal*) pays some positive attention to this aspect of industry and its growth. Pollution abatement could even, like defense, become a command sector and hence serve as a stabilizer against the fluctuations of the business cycles.

It is a widespread mistake to regard pollution abatement, and other measures to counteract environmental deterioration, as if they were in some sense less important than the production of the goods which cause the disutilities. We are not yet quite accustomed to the idea that the goods plus the disutility form a package which is worth less to us (it has less positive value) than the goods would be alone by themselves if they could be produced without generating disutilities. To this extent, industry without pollution abatement, for instance, is in fact less productive than it is conventionally credited with being. The cost of the goods was underestimated and not paid in full. Some of the costs are borne by contemporary people—and not necessarily in proportion to how much they consume of the goods—and some are deferred and borne by people later on, as in some cases when chemical dumps become more hazardous with time. Pollution control and other measures of environmental protection introduce again some such costs and force industry to produce a more valuable package. They also tend to force consumers to pay the environmental costs in proportion to how much of the goods they consume. The conflict between production and environment protection is thus apparent only, when we regard the national economy as a whole. There is also an element of conflict of distribution between rich and poor. The rich have more to lose and the poor more to gain from a sound environment. For the economy as a whole, environmental protection is part of a rational production package.

HIDDEN PRODUCTIVITY GAINS: COST OF PRODUCTION VERSUS VALUE IN USE

The overhead disutilities we have just discussed tend to make national product less valuable than it appears from conventional accounting measurements, and also somewhat differently distributed between the income classes of society. Against this stands a tendency to under-estimate real national product because of hidden productivity gains. They are hidden for two main reasons: the statisticians have not found any means of handling them, and people in general soon take improved conditions for granted and forget how it was before. Many technological advances are so great that their true scope can only be gauged with difficulty or not at all. We are referring now to the service rendered, while conventional accounts look at cost of production. For instance, a computer can do things which previously would have required large crews of clerks, if indeed they could be done at all. A teleprinter terminal, e.g. one receiving market news, does the work of three full-time clerks at a cost which is a small fraction of the paycheck of one clerk. Airplanes convey airmail on a scale that carrier pigeons never could have done, even at astronomic costs.

In many cases, the magnitude of the gain is overlooked because the old technology was too costly to contemplate for the jobs now done by the new technology. Market news transferred by telephone and taken down by stenographers served only a few large customers, while the teleprinters reach many more. The measurement and comparison is compounded by the different levels of wages over time. An example is the hand processing of complex statistical data for the German Census (1885 and later years). It assumed very low wages and hence represented much less value product than would have been credited to the same number of workers in recent time. On the modern scene, we must assume that electronic census processing replaces the high-paid workers of today, not the low-paid ones of a hundred years ago.

In each case of spectacular technological advance, conventional national-product accounting merely credits an advanced activity with its industrial opportunity cost. This means, what other products could have been turned out by using the same amount of input as in the new product, to make it and to keep in operation. What the new gadget replaces—potentially more often than actually—is not measured in national accounts. To all this comes one more motive making us forget: when something becomes cheap, it also tends to be used for cheap purposes. What it cost a dollar to compute in the 1950's now costs but a cent to compute; but then the new capacity may be used for purposes worth only a small fraction of the value of what was done with computer capacity when it was more expensive. Nowadays we often see computers used to solve silly problems. At the margin, use value will adjust to cost of production, but average cost of production has fallen much more than can be expressed in conventional accounting.

On a more trivial level, a new and improved floor wax, for instance, may render a better service than the old one, but at the same price. The difference is now labeled "qualitative" and the index numbers fail to capture it. The quantity aspect of the change is, of course, in the shorter time it takes to use the improved product, or in the longer intervals between its use.

For a multitude of reasons of these types, current rates of increase in national product are grossly understated. Measurement of utility created would show much higher rates of growth than those conventionally acknowledged. Recently the suggestion was made by a responsible statistician that the whole problem of low economic growth and slow productivity improvement in the 1970's may have been overstated because of the statistics' inability to measure improvements in electronic equipment, a leading sector in recent economic growth.

Again, as in the case of pollution and other disutilities, we have to ask about the social distribution of the gains, hidden or otherwise. People who get food stamps seldom own home computers. It may be that more accurate measurement of national product as utility would reveal sharper class cleavages in American society than we are aware of.

Turning now to the material conditions for unlimited economic growth, there are two major motives: population control, and development toward less materials exacting products.

POPULATION CONTROL

The demographic issue is relatively simple. On any given level of material consumption per capita, a given rate of population increase will necessitate at least the same rate of increase in the consumption of materials. If the per-capita material consumption standard is rising at the same time, total consumption of materials will grow even faster than population. And this factor will be stronger, the higher the level of per-capita materials consumption that has already been reached. At present, the slow rates of population increase in the rich countries cause a stronger drain on resources than does the more rapid population growth in the poor countries. The difference in the absolute level of per-capita resource consumption is that large. But given time, the material standards of the present low-income countries will rise and the more they do so, the more embarrassing will be the effect of continuing rapid population growth, by the accelerating depletion of resources which would follow.

The Conditions for Unlimited Economic Growth   135

You might object that, as the following pages will show, increasing substitution of materials and goods will eventually lessen the rate at which people draw on scarce resources. True as this is in general, it has less application to that part of the growth in demand which depends most directly on population growth. More people will need and demand more food, clothing, shelter, space heating and cooling, transportation and other necessities of life. And these necessities have less scope for substitution than do the luxuries and the cultural budget which tend to grow faster on higher income levels. Food has some scope for substitution, of vegetable protein as well as fat for those of animal origin, but this applies mainly to the already rich countries which consume large amounts of animal products. The vast majority of the world's people are already close to being vegetarians and most can never reach our level of consumption of foods of animal origin, so they will have little use for these substitutions either.

All told, the conclusion is inescapable: Unless the peoples of the earth come to terms with the problem of runaway population increase within the next few decades, there can be little hope of escaping or even postponing the resource catastrophy which the Club of Rome discussed.

This ought to answer one of the more far fetched objections to population control: that it would restrict (unfairly, to unborn generations) the "access to life" by limiting coming generations to smaller numbers than those that would be born under unlimited population increase. The opposite is rather likely to be true. Under unrestricted population increase, mankind would head for a catastrophy which would put a stop to further access to life, not many generations from now. But with a slowdown of the demographic trend and an eventual stabilization of the world's population, there is no particular limit on how many generations that may follow upon each other. Eventual access to life has a chance of being many times greater if the world settles down to long-term equilibrium in resource use. Accommodating to the level of energy use which can be obtained from solar applications, the limit set by fossil and nuclear sources will be lifted.

Under stable world population, there need not be any particular limit on the continued rise in real per-capita incomes. The terms for this need to be spelled out. Critical issues are in energy use, saturation of the demand for material goods, and substitution of materials, processes, and uses.

NO LIMITLESS ENERGY

The limits to fossil and nuclear energy sources are sometimes discussed as if all we need is to discover new large sources of these kinds. Deep-pressurized natural gas is hypothesized to exist in enormous quantities deep down—this would not really be fossil but a part of the planet's original endowment. Plutonium fission and fission of uranium bred from thorium, and fusion energy, have in turn been proposed as ultimate solutions to the energy problem for any foreseeable future. All of these hypothesized large energy sources would however lead us into problems even greater than those we seek to escape. Even if we had access to unlimited energy sources of a fund-resource character, such as the fossil and nuclear ones, we could never use them without limit. Burning of fossil hydrocarbons (including the hypothetical deep-pressurized "primal" gas though it may not really be fossil) would increase the carbon content of the atmosphere, provoking a "greenhouse" effect which has already been observed on a limited scale around large cities. If such climate modification were to become general, we might change the whole ecosphere in ways which are entirely beyond our control. Even a very high rate of heat released from nuclear sources, whether fission or fusion, could alter the thermal balance because the atmosphere can not rid itself of additional heat at just any rate, and least of all if the warmer climate were to bring more cloudiness.

Captured and re-cycled solar energy would represent no net addition either to atmospheric heat or to the air's carbon content. But under known and economically tested technologies there are limits to this. Green plants can only metabolize so much carbon, also because there is only so much to metabolize at any one time. Waterfalls, wind energy, tidal waves and other physical manifestations of energy originating in the sun are also finite and measurable, even though they continue indefinitely over time. Recent technology to produce hydrocarbon compounds from the atmosphere by aid of artificial (manufactured) chlorophylls appears technically accomplished. Like green biomass, this energy source would be ecologically benign. Whether it will ever produce commercial energy at costs within our economic reach, that we can not yet say. The same, of course, is true of the much heralded prospect of fusion energy.

As far as anyone knows, "unlimited energy" is therefore not part of the answer to our long-range problems. Intelligent curbing of the growth of energy use is an indispensable part of the solution. The eventual long-range solution of the energy problem will have to be in some self-renewing system of solar energy conversion which alone can become stable over an indefinite future.

For the same reasons, we also can not count on unlimited re-cycling of scattered materials such as scarce metals which we continue to disperse in small doses of throw-away objects. The reason is that all re-cycling uses energy and proportionately more, the more scattered the materials. The same holds for sources which are widely scattered in nature—the extreme case is gold in seawater. The need to hold down the use of energy also places limitations on the substitutions of materials, as far as large quantities are concerned.

DEMAND SATURATION

One reason why a stable population may stabilize its use of materials is that eventually there will be saturation of the demand for such goods. The demand curves will flatten out sooner or later.

The classical case is food. More than a century ago, a German statistician named Ernst Engel (not to be confused with Friedrich Engels, the socialist theoretician) discovered what is known as Engel's Law: with rising per-capita income, spending for food rises slower than total consumer spending. Demand will gradually shift toward foods of higher quality, and even that grows slower and slower. The total weight of food eaten will reach a physical maximum and then even go down somewhat because an easier life requires less body energy.

The same will eventually apply to housing, house heating and air conditioning, clothing, transportation, and so on. Obviously, when the number of cars becomes very large, not all of them could be used at the same time: even if the whole population were driving, no one could drive more than one car at a time. Such an extrapolation into the absurd may not sound very encouraging in itself, but at least it illustrates how the impact of continued population growth would be different from that of continued rise in per-capita income. The latter will pose less of a threat of resource depletion than would unlimited population growth.

The analogy with food consumption is more than casual. Chinese Buddhas were always pictured as very fat as well as benevolent, and in Europe around 1900 a prosperous man had to be on the plump side. The tradition of scarcity had bred gluttony. Abundance of food first made possible the ideal of a trim figure. Our current gluttony on matter and energy may also abate when we get far from the memories of past scarcities. But then we should get far from those memories—and continued social waste is less likely to accomplish a feeling of independence from want than is a rational resource and production policy.

Given a static or near-static population, even rising per-capita income levels may mean that demand for energy and materials will flatten out much earlier than would follow from extrapolation of trends that are current now. There are several reasons for such a reduction in the levels of energy use and materials use which are needed for a high and rising level of living. These reasons include more efficient use of energy and materials, substitution of less scarce materials for the more scarce ones, miniaturization of many engineering products, and a switch toward less materials exacting articles of consumption but which embody more and more complex designs which can produce more satisfaction for less materials use. These avenues toward reducing the energy and materials requirements are not always clearly separable, to a large extent they overlap and interact. We can only give examples; most readers will want to add some of their own.

SUBSTITUTION OF MATTER FOR MATTER

More economic use of materials is readily visualized in regard to energy. There are many economy measures which can be applied directly or indirectly in industry and even in agriculture (no-tillage cropping, wider use of nitrogen bacteria). There are above all—and especially so in the United States—two main areas of energy use which can be cut down drastically. The reader will have seen some indications of these already. One is in house heating (and air conditioning) by better insulation and more intelligent design and layout of buildings. The other is in use of mass transit instead of individual driving for commuting and other routine transportation of persons. Details are indicated in Chapters 3, 4 and 5 above. The policy outlook will be debated in the final two chapters below.

Substitution of materials and processes also can lead to large economies in the use of energy and materials. They should do so when the materials we now use become more expensive. When we look toward the future, we must of course use a bit of imagination to grasp some of the production possibilities that are waiting in the wings as consequences of technological advances already made. We should not fall into the trap of the Boston economist a hundred years ago who tried to estimate the effects of urbanization in America upon the demand for transportation in the cities—in terms of horses, oats, hay, and the land needed to grow these crops! The future can not be gauged on the basis of essentially the same factor and product mixes that we know from the present and the recent past. Some changes will be forced along by the new raw-material scarcities. Others will come as the outflow of continued technical ingenuity.

Good examples can be found in agriculture—generally not a science-fiction area. We have already the substitution of high-quality margarine for butter, as commented upon in Chapter 2. Synthetic milk and meat analogs may come to replace a large part of all that is now produced through animal husbandry. All of this will greatly relieve the ecological pressure of intensive land use as well as reduce the drain on energy. Eventually we may also get strains of non-leguminous crops, such as corn and wheat, capable of harboring nitrogen bacteria, which will save energy from nitrogen fertilizers. On the level of high-luxury consumption, agriculture and horticulture may produce very high-grade products without having to draw much more on resources than is true of less exquisite versions of the same food value or amenity. Variety improvements of fruits and vegetables could go that route rather than that of the hard tomatoes forced along for mechanical harvesting, and orchids take not much more glasshouse capacity than do many less enchanting flowers.

SUBSTITUTION OF DESIGN FOR MATTER

In industrial production there are of course many more possibilities than in agriculture. Here we should dispose of an error often made in debating the future of industry: when it can not be as energy intensive or as materials intensive as at present, the alternative is said to be backtracking toward more labor intensive methods of production. This would of course also mean retreating toward lower levels of real income, as is characteristic of labor intensive economic systems. Nothing could be more misleading than this assumption of higher labor intensity in the industry of the future. (The services are another matter—they should be made to absorb whatever surplus labor commodity production does not need). The specification of production inputs as materials (including energy) and labor, is far from complete. Any definition of capital which identifies it with its material bulk or its conventional market price (derived from cost of production) is unrealistic when production is thought of in terms of real utility. Both capital goods and goods intended for final use in consumption consist mainly of design— the ways matter is organized into products of varying complexity. Most of the design features nowadays are man-made rather than gifts of nature. The further development of industry will depend on increasing design intensity, as has already to a large extent happened in the past.

The point about design as an input factor should be obvious but is often overlooked. A heap of bricks and mortar can be used to build a cathedral or a jailhouse, a high-rise apartment building or a number of one-family dwellings. Each of these structures can also be built of something else than brick and mortar, such as pre-cast concrete slabs, for instance. In each case it is evident that the architect's drawing makes more difference than the choice of raw material. And so it goes with the whole gamut of modern industrial production: the increasing sophistication of design creates much more value than any raw material. The hardware used in a space rocket is the base on which millions upon millions of dollars worth of value product are generated. Energy concentrated in a laser beam can be used to do jobs which previously would have required much larger amounts of energy, if they were at all possible. Increasing design intensity—the use of more advanced and more efficient designs which are not necessarily more complex— will make industry produce more and more additional utility without for that sake drawing more on materials and energy. Again the several avenues of expansion mentioned above come to mind, especially those of making things more durable, applying more substitution of materials and processing, and miniaturization.

On the last point, the possibilities are extremely wide. As an example, let us discuss the development of document reproduction. Among the more appealing futurology excursions made lately is the forecast that sometime in the next century it will be possible within a middle-class income to own a piece of furniture which contains a microdot reader and enough microdot sheets to read off . . . all the books in the whole world, including the catalogs and whatever you need to find quickly what you are looking for (John Platt, The Step to Man). In terms of use value, such an asset is worth literally many millions of dollars in today's money, yet it may be within the reach of rather ordinary people.

At first blush this may sound very extreme indeed. On closer inspection it is less so. We already have high-fidelity gramophone records and cassette recordings which will let us listen to large orchestras in the quiet of our living rooms; the cost of hiring the orchestras for private enjoyment would of course be prohibitive for nearly all of us. Television similarly brings a wealth of filmed and soundtracked material into our homes at a cost, even if we paid for it directly, which would always be an extremely small fraction of the cost of obtaining the same satisfaction by the means that were conventional before the current technology.

ACCESS AND USE

Of course, access does not guarantee intelligent use. The garbage that fills large parts of television's program time merely points to the abundance which the medium represents, since it can be squandered so unabashedly; but other goods are squandered along with it. And all the groaning, moaning and moping which passes for music on American radio these days rubs in that the medium as such is not a message.

The parallels are many, and they include the many people who got so hooked on the automobile that they have to use it to go shopping two blocks away from their homes. Intelligent use depends on enlightened minds, and that does not come with the gadgets. Let a hog travel to Italy and he will still be a hog when he comes home again. The quality of consumption can not be separated from the quality of the consumer, and that leads us into the quality of education. We have argued, in a previous chapter, that organized education entails huge amounts of social waste by the skimpy results in terms of cultural quality as well as in the usually modest level of competence obtained for all the costs of the school system.

A typical instance of consumer quality was observed in a plush restaurant in San Diego, Cal., not long ago. The sunday lunch featured a vast smorgasbord table loaded with delicious dishes both hot and cold. Many more than anyone could try to taste, all exquisitely cooked and offered at a surprisingly modest price. There were not many takers. A family of five took a desultory look, then decided by the majority vote of the children (ages 8, 10 and 12) to skip the whole scene and go for a hamburger joint instead. The parents who caved in to the demand of immature minds did their offspring no favor. Neither do the schools which make their charges the standard rather than enforcing standards on them. And the media, essentially, have abandoned their logical role of leading the public's taste and instead concentrate on leading the public's money to the goods supplied by the highest-paying advertisers.

In a wider sense, the attainment of tomorrow's general affluence is threatened by the continuation of social waste. Technology will give us riches but the market turns too much of it into rags. The following two chapters will try to draw together the conclusions of this book by offering two separate perspectives on this facet of political economy.

Chapter 11
Back to Supply-Side Waste . . .

Social waste has to a large extent been due to resource owners stimulating more use of what they have to sell, such as minerals and other products of land. This sustains prices. Another way of obtaining such support of some prices is by keeping some resources out of competition, as in job discrimination which supports the price of manpower in favored categories. Such waste, often reckless, has been possible in America more than anywhere else. The penalties in this country were hard to perceive as long as the natural resources being wasted were abundant, and the demand for high-quality manpower as yet not very large. But now, the once lavish riches of America's high-grade fossil fuels (oil and natural gas) are beginning to run out. At the same time the need for highly qualified manpower begins to make discrimination by sex and "race" more and more patently absurd for purely material reasons. The weight of a highly complex defense budget also calls for better economizing, that is for cutting down on social waste. The agenda of the future, it would seem, should include national policies designed to address these new problems.

Instead, we now have national policies which under the label of "conservatism" try to turn the clock back on some of the modest progress made in the direction of a less wasteful economy. The current agenda includes reverting to "market forces" instead of economic planning, allowing entrenched interests to steer the future along the lines of the past. Conservation of resources is given second place to new production, even at sharply rising real cost. Economic stimulus is sought in "supply-side" economics of increased production running ahead of demand and of increased supply of capital hopefully encouraged by reduced Federal income taxes—even though some other taxes go up instead. At the same time defense expenditures are boosted at very high cost, with continued duplication of nuclear and conventional weapons. Objectives of social and economic equality are set aside or postponed, on the theory that "trickle-down" will help the poor by crumbs falling from the table of the rich, and that discrimination can be fought by means even less incisive than those which have had such difficulty getting results in the recent past.

All of this is supposed to be "conservative" in the sense that it should bring America back into closer similarity to its past, the time when this country first was shaped up from wilderness and chaos. This conservative agenda is hailed as undoing some of the alleged excesses of economic and social policies labeled "liberal", since the New Deal policy of the 1930's.

This chapter will discuss whether such policies are likely to conserve this Republic. Can the future be patterned on the past? The trends of social waste, and their consequences under current policies, should provide the answer.

BACK TO THE MARKET

A leading slogan in recent politico-economic propaganda is, "let the market handle it", or "rely on the private sector". What really is the market, and how private is the private sector?

Markets are not politically neutral. Unlike the forces of nature, those of the markets are not objectively given once and for all. The "economic climate" is not to be compared to the physical climate. Market fluctuations are not like rain and sunshine. Markets are artifacts, they are made by people and they can be changed by people. Often people do not know what they are doing when they create and maintain markets, but that does not render the market any less of an artifact. In central concerns such as monetary policy (the Federal Reserve system) or fiscal policy (the Office of Management and Budget), manipulation of markets is generally accepted. In such concerns, no modern government dreams of allowing things to drift by themselves, without systematic steering from the center.

The core difficulty about allowing market forces to decide the direction of economic events is that markets, far from representing the entire economy and polity in any objective way, instead represent the several interests which are strong in the current economic setup of a society. They represent these not in proportion to their significance for the future but in proportion to their inherited clout. Markets are inherently conservative, if it is conservative to want to go on as before. Saying "leave it to market forces" means accepting the economic structure as it is, as to composition between income groups, sexes, "races", and other subdivisions of society. Specifically, market forces would do little about institutionalized social waste for it is part of the market's economic power structure, it represents entrenched economic interests.

When openly faced with problems of social waste, market forces tend to work around these rather than trying to break them down. Market forces did not anticipate the oil crisis; they allowed it to steal upon us like a thief in the night. Market forces did next to nothing to break down discrimination against women and minorities, nor did they of their own accord do much about problems of hard-core poverty. Even margarine came to prevail over butter much slower than it might have if consumer welfare had been the leading economic principle. Entrenched interests did their best to retard a change which was beneficial to the general welfare. The same is repeated again and again when new products come into conflict with established ones. Retail outlets may simply not be forthcoming as in the case of vegetable milk substitutes which are only allowed a tiny market share as diet foods for those who can not tolerate natural milk. Conversely, "supply-side" marketing does not hesitate to push products which the public does not really want, such as the home computer which is a prestige item much more than a utility, at best premature for the current level of education.

BUSINESS AS GOVERNMENT

The ways in which strong market partners are able to force the events of the economy make us wonder, is the private sector always private? Is not private business sometimes a part of our system of government?

The case has been made above all in relation to the transnational corporations, some of which have been likened to sovereign states because they tend to escape the controls both of the government in their headquarters country and in several host countries. Their power derives not from guns but from money, economic leverage. The same of course is true of highly concentrated industry also within one country, especially a large one such as the United States. The oil majors come readily to mind. They have shaped energy policy for this country by their industrial concentration, by the size of the economic means assembled in their hands, and by the critical necessities represented by the energy sector. Outright lobbying is secondary to all those sources of economic power. No one can claim that their energy policy on behalf of the United States has been very beneficial. Steering by short-range motives of immediate profit, they allowed the oil-price shocks of 1973–74 and 1979–81. Because of their long-range interest in retaining most of the energy business in their own hands, they have done their best to delay the coming of substitute energy sources and also to delay more vigorous efforts to reduce the demand for oil, all of which would reduce their profits by reducing social waste. This is much more serious than delaying margarine for, unlike butter, petroleum will indeed run out one day; and our lives will then depend on new energy sources being there on time.

Another striking case of business as government is the automobile industry. For decades this industry ruled the country by its strength. Recently it has begun to do so by its weakness. The automobile industry exploits the fears of unemployment and the habituated thinking about the automotive sector as a growth engine indispensable to the economic health of the country, even after the demand for cars has begun to flatten out and part of the market has been conceded to foreign manufacturers.

In a naked display of economic power and of a will to economic conquest, one combination of automobile and oil interests began, in the 1920's, to buy up urban transit systems so they could either scrap them or switch them from electricity (trolley) traction to diesel engines, thus making one more outlet for an oil product. No countervailing force of matching strength was there to stop them.

Such virtually sovereign domains are still counted in the leading ideology as being in the "private sector", along with small shopkeepers and restaurateurs, struggling small-scale industrial innovators and ambitious service outfits. Giving blanket approval of the "private sector" guarantees the continuation of much of the social waste that goes on, allows it to run its course. Under current policy, for instance, the incipient transition to more mass transit (especially for commuting) has been halted and in part reversed, always because of the apparent lack of profit in a system which is stacked against the transit lines.

Evidently, the market mechanisms we are looking at have serious imperfections. These imperfections are not taken account of in the idealizing schemas of pure economic theory. Pointing to the superiority of American market economics over, say, the command economics of the Soviet Union, is not saying very much. The American system is without any doubt far better, but then it should be. Soviet socialism has created such a mess of built-in inefficiencies that we should not draw too much comfort merely from being better than that.

SUPPLY-SIDE CAPITAL

Part of the reasoning in supply-side economics is that the pool of savings available for investment is too small, it must be made larger by lowering the level of taxation.

On the lowering of the Federal income tax, official comments stress the alleged fact that it is across-the-board, it gives proportionately the same degree of tax relief to everyone. Even when the Federal income tax is looked at alone by itself, that statement is not entirely true. It holds for income levels up to $100,000, but not above that. Comparing the tax tables for 1980 and 1983 (the preliminary ones, distributed to help compute estimated tax payments), we find that in most income brackets the tax has been reduced by 18–19 percent, but more on the higher levels: at $200,000 in annual income, the tax relief is to the tune of 30 percent. This is because the highest marginal tax bracket was lowered from 70 percent to 50 percent, a proportionately greater reduction than in most tax brackets.

But that is not all, Part if not all of the tax relief (on the Federal tax schedule) is offset by increases of other taxes. These are mainly on the State and local levels but some are also Federal taxes. These taxes which are being increased are not progressive (as the Federal income tax) and so they hit people in the lower income levels harder. These people lose most if not all of their Federal tax relief in this way. The higher income people, by contrast, get to keep most of the Federal tax relief. To compound it, the large Federal budget deficit leads to higher interest rates, that is to higher incomes for people who have money to invest, either in Federal bonds or elsewhere. Those who have no spare funds get no part of this Federal bonanza flowing from the current fiscal policy.

Despite this favoring of high-income people, there have been few signs of any incipient investment boom following the tax changes. The first that was heard on the news after the first round of tax reduction was about brisk business in the trade with furcoats and other luxury consumer goods. There has also been a wave of American tourists going abroad which again is of interest mainly to the affluent and hardly a contribution to saving and investment at home.

Even as the much commented-upon economic recovery makes the news in 1983, investment appears to be lagging. Retail sales are up. Those receiving high interest on their savings find that they have more money to spend. The recession left a backlog of unfulfilled demand. The unending chain of sales-at-reduced-prices leaves us wondering how much of the previous inflation reflected exaggerated markups of prices intended for such spectacular apparent price reductions, deliberately planned to be launched when the business outlook appears favorable for them.

But capital formation is still not picking up. Manufacturers' expectations of investment for 1983 have been below those for last year ever since the winter, and they still are. So what is wrong with supply-side capital theory?

Part of the explanation must be in the huge Federal deficit which forces the Treasury to borrow at high interest. Contrary to what some of the commentators lead the public to believe, real interest rates have not gone down as much as has conventional inflation—these real rates are still very high. And, what is almost never mentioned, high rates of interest are in fact a variety of inflation—they are inflation in the cost of capital. The real rate of interest is the difference between the nominal rate of interest and the rate of inflation.[1] The real rate never exceeded 3 percent in any year between the late 1930's and the late 1970's. The size of the U.S. economy doubled from 1940 to 1960 and once more from 1960 to

---

1. Usually, we take a shortcut: the real rate is taken as the difference between the nominal rate and the rate of inflation. The rate should really be figured as follows:

1980, thus a fourfolding in as many decades. This means long-term economic growth (as conventionally measured) in those forty years—recessions and all—at a compound rate of 3½ percent per year. Evidently, high rates of real interest are not a requisite for healthy economic growth.

Using as base statistics the "prime rate" as shown in the financial data, and the implicit deflator of the national accounts to measure inflation, we find that real interest rates rose over the 3-percent level for the first time in decades in 1979 to reach 3.7 percent, reflecting the onset of the second oil-price crisis. They continued to rise to 5.5 percent in 1980, 8.6 percent in 1981, and to a historic high of 9.8 percent in 1982. In the first quarter of 1983 we found "only" 6.9 percent but this has risen since then—not only did the prime rate go up again in the summer of 1983, but as the rate of inflation fell even more, the real rate of interest rose more than the prime rate.

All of this recent interest-rate history is without precedent since the height of the Great Depression, in the early 1930's, when real interest rates for a short time rose (exceeding the record of 1982). This was largely due to deflation (rising purchasing power of money) and it did not last long.

As the Federal Treasury borrows, investible funds keep on earning high interest on bonds and treasury bills, rather than factories and trade. As long as this goes on, there will be no large supply of funds for investment. This holds with a vengeance, for if business really decided to step up their rates of real investment, they too would contribute to bidding up the rates of interest. Thus an incipient investment boom would be choked off by its own momentum.

It remains to ask whether the tax-relief, supply-side capital theory was even elementarily right to begin with.

$$\frac{1 + \text{nominal interest rate}}{1 + \text{rate of inflation}} = 1 + \text{real interest rate}$$

The difference between this answer and that from the shortcut is small when the rates are low, but when they are high, the above formula gives a more accurate answer.

RICH SAVERS, POOR WASTERS?

The conventional wisdom is that rich people save a larger part of their incomes than do people on lower income levels, and that therefore the rate of savings in the economy will be higher when the rich get richer.

The first part of the statement is a trivial truth, but only in the static sense. As a description of what goes on in a given situation, it is true to say that the rich do indeed save a larger percentage of their incomes than do the poor or even the middle classes. This follows from the shape of a number of demand functions for consumer goods. We have already mentioned (in Chapter 10) the demand function for food, known as Engel's law. The higher the income, the lower the percentage of all consumption spending that is for food. The same holds, with variations, for other necessities of life such as clothing and housing. Logically, then, more money will be left over for saving at the higher income levels, and so it is. The static truth can be verified from any number of censuses and surveys.

But that is not the whole story. The conventional wisdom also wants us to believe that the rule holds in the dynamic sense: make the rich richer and there will be more savings. In this dynamic formulation, the statement is a fallacy. It does not have any good evidence to bear it out; there is in fact evidence to the contrary. If it had been true that the more unequal the income distribution the larger would be the rate of savings in the country, then the rates of savings would be higher in Latin America than elsewhere in the world, for those countries have the most extreme inequalities of both income and wealth. The result is in fact quite otherwise: rates of savings in Latin America are not particularly high, and the economic as well as the sociopolitical performance of the region is far from encouraging.

The prime cause of these dismal results in Latin America is in conspicuous consumption, an imperfection to economic theory first signalled by Thorstein Veblen just before the turn of this century. When the rich become very rich, many of them lose the motivation for high savings, and indeed for maximizing conventional income. Leisure and unproductive consumption take on more scope. The trouble is that in a society where this is an important feature, the upper middle classes also feel motivated to emulate the very rich, as an element in social competition. The complaint has been made time and again (as, e.g., in Colombia several years ago) that the shortfall of savings really was due to the squandering habits of the upper middle class rather than those of the super rich because these upper-middle class people, collectively, have more of the country's income than the very rich. This overlooks the force of example. The "climate for savings" is not very good when a life of unearned leisure ranks high on the scale of social values.

In several countries in western Europe, and also in Japan, large savings available for investment have been possible in a large part because also the middle classes—low as well as high, and also many "blue-collar" workers—have been in the habit of saving and have had the inducement to it. Those are the people whose savings habit ought to be fostered. The recent tax changes, by favoring above all the rich, are not encouraging a more broad based increase in the rate of savings. Moving us into the direction of the kind of social stratification that prevails in Latin America will not be of service to American society.

The saving habits among the middle classes in this country are also not channelled in the direction of productive real investment. Tax incentives and other public policies continue to favor consumer spending on precisely those goods—that is houses and cars—which compete the most directly with industry for investment goods and funds.

Favoring the rich at the expense of the poor and the lower middle classes will have yet another negative consequence for the continued development of the economy. Increased inequality will also mean greater economic power to resource owners because it means that more of the social product becomes distributed in a way that rewards capital more and labor less. Rewarding capital more will lead to higher returns on natural resources. Higher returns on natural resources will give the owners of such resources a further motive (and a freer hand) in promoting social waste of products originating in natural resources (such as food, oil and minerals) because this will further strengthen the income as well as the power of the resource owners.

ENERGY AND CAPITAL

Current policy includes among its ingredients an attempt at disregarding the energy problem. This was announced, rather loudly, in the election campaign of 1980: the energy problem, we were told, would be solved by leaving it to private enterprise. There was supposed to be enough oil in America's earth to make us independent of oil imports; so the party line ran. As election propaganda it went down well with the electorate: what would be more pleasant than to believe that a deadly danger hanging above our heads does not really exist? A high government official, early in 1981, also made the comment that it was "a nice change of pace" not to have to talk so much about energy. The trouble is, of course, that the problem itself will not go away just because it is told to.

In accord with the new signals, decontrol of the prices of domestic petroleum was hastened: it was three-quarters complete at the end of 1980 and the remainder, due by September of 1981 was moved up to January of the same year. Decontrol of natural-gas prices is continuing as intended. Previous official policy to steer away from petroleum imports was shelved because imported oil was found to be cheaper. This is an interesting comment on the prospects for more domestic oil production which had been riding so high in 1980. The oil-and-gas drilling boom of 1980–81 turned out to be a disappointment. This happened only months after the government took office which had rested its policy choice on this premature promise of success.

When oil prices then turned downward in 1982, because of the oil glut prompted by the worldwide (and including the U.S.) recession, things got so bad for the decontrolled domestic petroleum sector that the recession even reached into Texas.

The downturn of international oil prices reflected recession which in turn had been triggered foremost by high oil prices, not by the policies of the previous administration. Nor can the current administration take credit for the fall in oil prices any more than it is inclined to take the responsibility for the recession. It is in any event likely that the recession was made worse by the policies followed in 1981 and 1982. It is predictable that, as economic activity picks up, so will the demand for oil. If the economic recovery continues much beyond the pre-recession level of per-capita national product (and we are just barely there, end of 1983), demand for oil will again boost its price and send us back to where we were before the recession. Price pressure from the energy sector, including consequent price pressure on physical capital, will then choke off the recovery. How can anything else be expected when the ultimate cause of the recession—in energy prices—had been overlooked?

The case of physical capital becoming more scarce and more expensive because of energy costs, was explained in Chapter 3. It is doubtful that the country can continue to carry an energy budget of this scope indefinitely, along with the kind of defense budget which appears inevitable for the foreseeable future.

But that is not all. The real oil crunch is yet to come. The Department of Energy may have been slated for scrapping under the present market minded administration, but it continues to turn out scenarios for future supply and prices of oil which ought to be the basis for a policy quite different from what we have. Beyond 1990, the projections tell us, both domestic and foreign oil supplies will be going down; the price of oil will be rising steadily through the decade, reaching the double (or more) of our present real-term oil-price level in just a decade. Doing next to nothing about this now is to assure very hard times for some future President to preside over. (Congress may still include many of its current members). The current policy of relying on the market does not work, it only loses us precious time which we are unlikely to be able to buy back. Replacement energy sources, of whatever description, will take time to build up to the quantities that will be required to replace oil and gas. The matter gets complicated by the logistics of accumulating large volumes of physical capital which can not always be accelerated at will, least of all with the kind of capital costs which already now are caused by the energy problem. All of this can only get worse by the time the oil crunch hits us in earnest.

MONEY AND GOODS

Devoid of any innovative spirit, current economic policy relies on inherited concepts and habits of thought even to the point that money is regarded as the substance of the economy. Money is not; goods and services are. Money is just a mechanism of exchange. It appears to individuals as a completely homogenous entity, freely exchangeable between alternative uses. A dollar is a dollar is a dollar. This laymen's experience is not always valid in social account. There we must recognize that spending money on defense hardware affects the economy in ways which are quite different from the effects of spending on food for the poor. Defense spending addresses different sectors of the economy than does food spending, and the consequences for scarcity and cost of capital, for instance, are also quite different. These differences in the impacts on economic sectors are especially important when the government sectors are changing in their proportions: expanding defense expenditures can not be paid for by reducing social programs. It only seems that way when fiscal policy concentrates its attention on money flows and forgets about the incidence on economic sectors. Thus it appears that the administration forgets not only the low employment effect of defense contracts (a point sometimes made by the political opposition) but also about the effects on the markets for scarce physical capital and on the distribution of income in society which becomes more unequal when capital intensive defense expenditures are maximized.

There are similar differences within private spending. As long as this concentrates on houses and cars, with their consequences for streets, roads and other utilities, consumer spending will have quite different effects on the economy than if more were spent on health care, light recreation, and culture. The diversity of money should be evident already from the different levels of cost-of-living, and the different rates of inflation, between parts of the country.

No such effects of varying economic structure are admitted in current economic policy. Economic expansion continues to emphasize automobiles and housing construction regardless of their impact on energy use and capital markets. These sectors of private spending are the most interest-rate sensitive (read: the most capital intensive) sectors of the civilian economy, exceeded only by the energy sector itself and the command sector of defense procurements.

A WORSENING SOCIAL STRUCTURE

No rhetoric about tax policy can undo the fact that social cleavages are worsening under current economic policy. Why else would it be so hard to fight discrimination at all levels? One-tenth of the work force (not even counting the "discouraged" workers who escape the statistics) is out of regular earning sources. An estimated one-fourth of America's children are said to be growing up in poverty—discrimination against women at many levels contributes a good deal to this result. Important parts of the nation's human potential are being neglected. The hope that rising affluence among the already affluent will "trickle down" to the poor is vague in expected timing and unsubstantiated in scope.

Nor is any relief in sight. Apologists for current policy emphasize time and again that unemployment is the last indicator to improve during economic recovery. Only seldom is it admitted that unemployment tends to go up more than it goes down. The record of the 1970's points to a steady long-term upward trend for chronic unemployment. "Full employment" in the United States used to be counted as a level of 4–5 percent unemployment. In Europe, it was assumed that full employment would mean 1–2 percent unemployed which was labeled "frictional unemployment", referring to people moving between jobs. But now we are told that the United States should count 6–7 percent unemployment as "full employment". How it could be called that is mysterious, unless the statement is an admission that the economy no longer is capable of using all its people, not even in times of normal prosperity.

This upward trend in unemployment is what we should expect from the increasing capital intensity of the economy which has been rendered more extreme by the energy problem and how it was handled. Energy is a very capital intensive sector and it has been allowed to retain most of its inherited scope in the face of rising capital intensity, thus now drawing larger parts of all national product into its service. Without recognizing and acting upon this connection between energy cost, capital cost and unemployment, the syndrome of the 1970's and early 1980's can only be expected to continue and to get worse. Economic recoveries such as those of 1975–77 and 1983 will be increasingly shallow because they are recoveries for an economy from which more and more people are excluded. The country can not thrive and prosper, and in the end not even defend itself, unless all its people have reasonable access to the sources of prosperity.

WISHFUL THINKING, VESTED INTERESTS, AND INERTIA

What we now have as official policy is leading the country toward more of the problems which brought its progress to a standstill. Only re-emphasizing the old *modus operandi* of the economy, without serious innovation and rejuvenation, is not to "conserve" it, except as things are conserved in a museum. Ossifying old bones is no way to health and vigor. Rather than preserving American society, the kind of "reconstruction" tried here can just lead us down a blind alley, straight into nothing.

The main obstacles hindering rational reforms in America's energy system and general economic structure are wishful thinking, vested interests, and the inertia of set habits. The social waste which has its extreme case in past and present misuse of petroleum has deep roots in the American attitude which says that we will always find a way out of all difficulties. Human ingenuity will do it. In a curious way, this reference to ingenuity in general tends to become void of ingenuity in the specific. Assuming that market forces will solve problems for us in ways which are to their short-run disadvantage, is certainly disingenious. For the scale and scope of the problems which social waste has saddled upon us, our ingenuity must find ways also through political innovation.

Chapter 12
. . . Or Forward to a Sane Society?

Past habits have left this country with a large syndrome of social waste. This has many interlocking features, rendering all solutions complicated because they have to be complex. Isolated policy departures are likely to backfire or be deflected back into the main pattern of wasteful resource use. Current policy does not even acknowledge the problem, much less do anything about it. Amid ambitious efforts (of questionable efficacy) to cut out many small cases of waste and fraud in the use of public funds, we see no attempt at coming to grips with the large causes of social waste. To the contrary, current policy, in the name of conventional conservatism, makes the inherited problems worse. From oil, cars and city slums, through drugs and routine education all the way to civil rights and the poverty problem, current policy makes us lose time. Time to find solutions, and time to implement them, neither of which can be accelerated at will just because a long looming crisis becomes overt.

Social waste, as we have seen, reflects pervasive market imperfections which prevent the economic process from working to the benefit of the whole country and all its people. Rather than blaming anyone in particular, we should look at the system—we must see how it works as a system. Individual firms, even the very large ones, only do what comes naturally in their business situation. Let us see how the system could be made to work better.

A MARKET CONCEPT OF PLANNING

A call for national economic planning does not have to mean a shift in the economic system. Rather than discussing the concepts of nineteenth century Socialist thinking, which have long proved their practical failure, we might contemplate the notion of "guided market economy" which was the watchword in the economic reconstruction of West Germany after World War II.

What American private business does well, is to run the businesses; what it does not do at all well, is to run the country. The latter requires unified economic policy objectives and a balancing of conflicting interests. To recognize that the national interest may in fact be different from the interest of General Motors, does not logically have to require measures directed specifically at General Motors. In the broad sense in which we discuss national policy here, the "common interest" has always been recognized as a legitimate area for the public powers to act on.

An adversary relationship between business and government can be viewed as a facet of our political system of "checks and balances" or "division of powers". In contrast to Socialism, it offers some protection against any extreme concentration of power, economic or otherwise. The argument runs both ways: government should not own business but neither should business have undue influence over government. The legislative branch must have the ultimate say in mediating conflicts between private and public interests.

We already have a great deal of economic regulation in this country. Most of it is short-range in intent and much of it runs at cross purposes. It does not add up: we have many policies but no coherent national economic policy. An over-all statement of what the political powers want the economy to accomplish, if convincingly displayed and consistently enforced, would in a sense give private enterprise more freedom to operate because they will face less uncertainty than with today's many conflicting piecemeal regulations.

The following will propose some of the policies which may prove necessary to reverse the dangerous trends that are under way. Although socio-political motives are mentioned time and again, we want to emphasize here, once more, that the necessities which have to be met are economic necessities. The removal or at least the sharp reduction of social waste will be beneficial in many ways, but it is first of all needed to set the economy on a long-term path of future growth which need not be interrupted by man-made crises.

OIL, CARS AND CITIES:
THE ECONOMIC EQUIVALENT OF WAR

Years ago, a President suggested that the energy problem in America was "the moral equivalent of war". The measures suggested in pursuit of this slogan were so modest that a major newspaper felt motivated to ask, on its editorial page, "the moral equivalent of what?"

America's political history shows a consistent tendency to avoid facing a crisis until it has come so close that it is perceived by a large part of the public. Thus it was with the long simmering Union crisis leading to civil war, and thus it was also with the Great Depression, warnings for which were apparent already to President Coolidge. Yet nothing was done until each of these two crises came to a head. Only then, on those two rare occasions, did this Republic deliberately elect strong national leadership.

The energy crisis is not now widely perceived as a crisis. It has been in the making since the 1950's, and its has caused severe economic dislocations which are far from being overcome. The current inaction on energy policy, inaugurated with great emphasis in the Republican election campaign of 1980, also means that we are losing precious time because nothing much is done to neutralize the crisis which is looming only a few years up ahead. The overt appeal to wishful thinking which is the current administration's stock-in-trade is so easy to use here because of the public's emotional reactions to anything that concerns transportation. We urgently need a shift in government stance to emphasize, with more convincing argument than so far have been used, the meaning and the seriousness of the energy problem.

The syndrome of automobile over-use, oil waste, traffic congestion, and over expansion of urban areas followed by premature decline in older city areas, consists of interlocking features which can not be broken by piecemeal economic measures, much less by moral exhortation. This part of the American economy needs major surgery, by means similar to some of those which occur in wartime. The object lesson is loud and clear in the historical statistics: during 1942–45, car making in the United States came to a virtual standstill, the car fleet declined, and passenger railway transportation reached historical heights.

The central lever which will control both traffic, fuel use, and city layout is the parking system. It was mentioned in the chapter about traffic: this kind of control is low cost, easy to enforce, and highly efficient.

We had a case in point in the town where I lived several years ago. A residential area near its university campus had become congested with commuter cars being parked all day long during the work week. Commuter cars lined the streets bumper to bumper, local residents could not get in edgewise either for emergency vehicles, routine service calls, or incidental private visits. Eventually a city ordinance was passed which prohibits on-street parking between 3 a.m. and 10 a.m., Monday through Friday. Exceptions are granted against a substantial rental fee, and parking fines are stiff. Police are instructed to make exceptions for service vehicles designated as such. The effect of the ordinance was immediate and enduring: the commuter cars vanished as if they had been blown away.

This technique of controlling traffic by controlling parking is far preferable to high gasoline prices. Gasoline may have to become more expensive in the future just because of rising supply costs, but these gradual price increases will not wean many people away from routine driving. Most drivers will simply get used to the higher prices and learn to save on something else, an attitude which will make the energy-waste syndrome in traffic even deeper entrenched, as if in its own ruts. Gasoline prices much higher than prospective costs—by high taxes, as in Europe—are not very desirable in this stage of American economic development. They would be likely to have more effect in reducing pleasure driving which is legitimate luxury, and less on commuting and routine shopping which is where intensive use of the car becomes social waste. Moreover, such very high gasoline prices are likely to bring back some of the class consciousness which once was a powerful booster for the car system—"keep up with you-know-who". Either way, very high fuel prices will at best be a very slow and tortuous route toward more concentrated city layout and less wasteful traffic.

Parking controls, by contrast, can give the impetus to far reaching changes in both fuel use, traffic patterns, and city layout within a short stretch of years. The question is not about their efficacy if used, but of the political difficulty in getting them accepted. This is where a strong policy formulation such as "economic equivalent of war" may help by rubbing in how serious the matter is.

It can be done in not very many years, but it can not be done over night. The Federal government could take a strong lead by a phased withdrawal of parking areas for its employees. This is not as novel as some people may think. Both NASA and the Pentagon are reported to be supplying parking space for only a fraction of their staffs, thus forcing many employees to go to work by means other than individual driving. Withholding space would also raise fewer legal questions than the attempt once made to have Federal employees pay more for their parking spaces. At the very least, the government could begin by no longer supplying any parking spaces to new employees, except those who are paraplegic or whose duties require car transportation. Next, a phased program of withdrawal of parking rights also from other able-bodied employees would be announced well enough in advance so that everyone could adjust, either by discovering where the mass transit is or by relocating their places of residence. In the meantime, of course, mass transit lines would develop more frequent schedules, sometimes also new service routes, to meet the increased demand for their service. The Federal government can already make a difference in places where it is a large employer. It can further negotiate with the State governments to make similar arrangements for their employees, which for instance include all the State universities. State governments could then also take steps to persuade local governments to do likewise. In private business, the government could use a combination of taxing parking spaces (as a luxury tax) and applying its other economic levers such as government contracts and tax provisions in favor of industry.

In routine shopping, the long-term alternative should be to redirect shopping toward more concentrated locations and with less use of individual cars. The difficulty is greater here than in the case of commuting, for a necessary complement is in more home delivery of articles which are bulky, heavy, or demand careful handling. We habitually get home delivery of milk, liquor, flowers and . . . pizzas (at 1 car-mile per pizza). The reason we don't get home delivery of kitchen towels and toilet paper, water melons and dog-food, or fresh bread and canned foods, is that supermarkets do not practice home delivery and probably could not start it very easily. The arrangements would have to be such that they can be handled by the generally rather low quality personnel who work as checkout clerks. Why many of these clerks are so hapless about simple handling chores which their predecessors in family stores carried out quite well is a problem related to the quality of mass education.

This is another case of large-scale social waste which on this point impinges very directly on the functioning of market arrangements. But once some of the heavier and bulkier goods are home delivered—on standard schedules, serving many customers in one trip, like the drycleaners—the rest of routine shopping may very well be done by travelling on mass transit, anyone can carry a bag or two on the bus. And with buses and transit trains running more frequently, there need be no real loss of efficiency or convenience.

Such reforms of the shopping system would have profound effects on the urban system. Downtowns could prosper again, reviving the atmosphere of social contact which is largely lost in today's abstractly efficient (but humanly inefficient) system of mass goods merchandising. Some peripheral shopping centers could continue to function for a time, with bus instead of car traffic, until such time that their buildings can be deployed for other uses; warehousing is an obvious alternative.

Renewed vitality of downtown areas would also be the starting point for reversing many of the destructive effects of the overgrown traffic system. All the consequences of central-city decay, including slum formation, ingrained poverty, drug culture and organized crime, would also become less intractable when the central city is again an economic center with much to lose from not enforcing its laws including those of economic and social justice and of education and health care in the wide sense of both terms. The city will have less social waste because it will be more efficient.

But it is evident that none of this can be made acceptable to the public unless the changes which are perceived as short-run losses are understood in their context of a grand scheme of long-range improvement.

Parallel with action on traffic, something will have to be done about real-estate taxation, and about "red-lining" of declining city areas by banks and insurance companies. The ad-valorem real-estate tax has been debated so long that its negative effects must be assumed to be well known, and it should be time to tone down this type of tax, or at least to re-direct it toward the land (and location) component rather than the improvements. As fixed costs, the real-estate taxes are hard to bear both for businesses and individuals who happen to have had a bad year for whatever reason. Red-lining, the power of banks and insurance companies to refuse credit and insurance to perfectly sound properties which happen to be located in declining neighborhoods, means placing the power of city planning in the hands of those corporations. Somehow or other, this power will have to be subordinate to the will of the community, both at the municipal and the neighborhood levels.

EQUALITY OF RIGHTS: A MATTER OF LAW AND MONEY

This set of problems is usually treated as a matter of justice toward individuals; and so it is also, of course. But here we emphasize the economic aspects of discrimination. This may be decisive for any possibilities of solving these problems, for experience shows that institutional remedies alone—just plain law and order—have not done the job.

The intent of the law has been there since the beginning of this Republic. It is sobering to contemplate how easily the principles of the Constitution were disregarded in favor of economic group interests, real or perceived. Take for instance the slavery debate before 1861. The Declaration of Independence states in no uncertain terms that all men are created equal and have God-given rights including that of liberty, and then some. Yet, men with a claim to honesty and integrity could stand there and contend without blushing that black men were not to be considered men. Knowing the truth did not help when the slave owners' perceived interest was to waste the asset which the black population could have been. In constitutional law, there never was any basis for slavery, any more than for lynchings—both were equally contrary to both law and order.

The same applies to women's rights. Looking back on all the nonsense that was once spoken and written against women's suffrage, one overwhelming fact stands out. Women' suffrage, all the time, had the same basis in American constitutional principle as the independence of the United States: No taxation without representation. Many women paid taxes early on. They were no more represented by male relatives or employers than the people of Massachusetts were represented by King George III.

There never was any basis in law for excluding women from the vote, or from any other civil rights, any more than there was a legal basis for slavery in a country of civil freedoms. The reason the Equal Rights Amendment is necessary is because of the false representation of the Constitution as a men's charter only—witness the suffrage amendment which rubs in rather than remove this misrepresentation. As with women's suffrage, all the propaganda against the ERA has not come up with a single argument which stands up to logical scrutiny. The cause of all this nonsense is, as with slavery, in the economic interests who want to go on exploiting—and wasting—women's labor.

In the future, each delay in civil rights and freedoms for women and minorities will be looked upon with as much contempt as we feel for those who once defended slavery and denied women the right to vote. But none of this is likely to tip the scales in the near future. Self-interest and inertia are equally blinding. In this country, as experience shows, money talks louder than ethical and legal principles. This is why it can not be over-emphasized that discrimination is economically destructive to the life of the nation. It is unpatriotic, and it can not in good logic be called conservative either.

To outshout the voice of money, a policy of enlightening all sides to the controversy is not enough. There must also be economic penalties on the wrongdoers, taking away from them the gains they may have secured (or wanted to secure) by discrimination. Fines must be high enough to deter both employers and unions and whoever else might be concerned, and the amounts of the fines must be made public as a measure of preventive justice.

POVERTY: RESOURCE WASTE AND RIOT HAZARDS

We have already explained why and how widespread poverty hurts society as a whole, not just the individuals concerned. Distribution of income affects the incentives of individuals to move upward in society, and extreme inequality blunts these incentives (chapter 8). Extreme and widespread poverty also poses a threat to peace and security in the community. We have also disposed of an argument often used to defend wide inequalities of income, the purported higher savings rates in very unequal societies which turned out to be an illusion (Chapter 11). It remains to pull together the policy conclusions from these observations on the political economy of poverty.

It is evident that society has an interest in keeping inequalities of income from becoming very wide. Some inequality is needed to maintain the incentive for upward mobility which is desirable if society is to have the full benefit of its talent pool. But too much inequality will have the opposite effect. The balance is an empirical problem, not one of pure theory. Societies and areas where existing inequality does not obstruct upward (and downward) mobility will be the norm.

Considering the several aspects of the poverty problem, including the hazard to property from large numbers of potentially riot prone proletarians, it is logical to re-emphasize the graduated income tax which has been watered down in recent tax policy. It is logical because those with very high incomes have more at stake in the continued economic health of the country and the continued security of their property. The argument can also be made that very high incomes are in part due to luck—especially the luck of advancing to one or another among the rare high "positional goods" such as the star effect in the world of entertainment or the economic leadership positions based on inherited wealth. Taxing very high incomes at rates much higher than those of ordinary incomes is therefore only belated justice.

The income tax has of course also the advantage over other taxes that year by year, it is better in proportion to the ability to pay. The contrast with the property tax is extreme, but also sales taxes have a tendency to weigh heavier on people who have difficulty affording them.

DRUGS AND DISCIPLINE:
THE SOCIAL EQUIVALENT OF PEACE

The failures of drug repression in recent time are as spectacular as that of prohibition against alcohol. The attempts at legislating against sin leave behind problems worse than those to which the repressive legislation is addressed. The conclusions extend beyond the drug problem, into other varieties of morality by fiat.

We have already shown (Chapter 6) that the net result of the drug campaigns is negative. Hence, all the costs of drug repression are wasted, and many more lives are destroyed by the powerful drug-trading criminal organizations which only thrive on the attempts at repression. The lesson should have been learned already in the 1920's, with alcoholic beverages. When a vice is widely cherished, the State can not fight it with police measures without turning into a police state, in itself a failure in a free society. Much as the clearheaded among us dislike drug use (including the use of alcoholic beverages as intoxicants rather than as a mere spice), it is only fair to recognize that drug abuse represents attempts at coping with life-stresses many people find hard to tolerate. Rather than attacking symptoms, a policy against drug use should be directed against underlying causes by making life more livable, as well as toward penalizing the consequences of drug use which pose dangers to other people. Tidying up social waste, especially that connected with city slums and widespread poverty without hope, would certainly help. At the upper end of the income scale, cocaine use in recent years points to complicated problems of wealth without normal self discipline. Across all social strata, education for individual fulfillment rather than for routine course work could reduce the tendency to escape into the sickly dream world of drugs.

The first thing to do must be to de-criminalize the mere use of drugs. "Controlled substances" are a bad joke anyway—they are all running out of control. Letting the common user off the hook will reduce the support of the drug dealers among the population and will let many more individuals testify in court against the criminal drug traders. With some legal access to their drugs, for "bona-fide addicts" as in England for instance, and at cost, the economic base for illegal drug trade would also be weakened. This would leave the criminal organizations less economic muscle with which to enforce their perverted will on society as a whole.

At the same time, something should be done about over-use of medicines. The pharmaceutical industries do not seem eager to reduce their profits by pointing out the long-term hazards of habitual use, or of using several different medicines at the same time. If medical professionals would be more consistently explicit in advising against always "fighting" minor pains by strong medication ("the strongest pain relief you can buy without a prescription"), they might do more good for the health of the people at large than is done by a small number of widely publicized organ transplants.

The drug prohibition syndrome should warn us also against legislation on morality. This is beyond the power of a free society to enforce. The self-styled "moral majority" (which may be neither, in fact) would, if it succeeded in some of its stated purposes, become the moral equivalent of civil war. Whatever their rationale, they could never enforce their will on a divided public. Amid sharpened cleavages between opposing camps, politicking moralists would only succeed in inflicting immense costs in the form of social waste for futile attempts at enforcement.

EDUCATION, RESEARCH AND CULTURE: PURPOSE OVER PAYCHECK

The education syndrome is not unique to this country, but it is more extreme here than elsewhere. When a system is wasteful, it tends to be more so when there is more to be wasted. Stultifying classroom routines tend to trap individuals—both teachers and students—to the point where they lose sight of how much easier it is to study alone and to learn individually.

The way out has in part been sketched in Chapter 7. It does not include "merit pay" for schoolteachers, because this would risk too much to reward those who parrot the conventional wisdom according to their principals, and it could demoralize those whose more unusual merits are not so easily recognized. Maintaining a good teaching staff does require decent pay, including the reasonable certainty that it will not be eroded by inflation or muscled out by the union power of janitors or the market value of gas station attendants. Decent dependable pay is the basis for professional integrity in a profession relying greatly on imponderables. Integrity also requires freedom from non-professional interference. Only then can gifted teachers be free to seek the non-material reward of pride in achievements—the achievement of more learning among their pupils. Those who can not inspire learning should be doing something else, such as maintaining order in a reading room.

Purpose over paycheck needs to be stressed also in other areas of cultural life. The research establishment, for instance, is much too prone toward "empire building". A research director's prestige as well as his salary may depend—as in any bureaucracy—on how much he spends rather than on how much he produces. How else can we explain the size of the vivisection enterprise in this country—the torturing and killing of some one hundred million laboratory animals every year in more or less medically oriented research (including "smoking dogs", and tests of cosmetics), when the total results of all this research are so uncertain as to what they mean to people? Our species has some unique features, after all, and results from animal research are seldom applicable right away. Thalidomide, the ill-fated tranquilizing drug aimed at pregnant women, would never have been let loose to produce eight thousand crippled children if it had not been declared "safe" by animal experimentation.

These remarks are not aimed solely at medicine. The economics professions might be sobered by their difficulties in explaining the economic changes of the last ten years, into considering also the economics of economics: the least-cost principle requires us to use the most economical means we can find for whatever it is we are trying to prove. On this test, a good deal of economic literature will be found wanting. We are just now meeting the test of a world in transition. It is the transitions that need our help—the static equilibria can take care of themselves whether we are able to explain them or not.

As in school teaching, the university establishment might be more productive if its creative forces were left free to work without having to meet some kind of evaluation day by day and year by year. The endless search for articles to publish, and for research dollars to spend, too often get in the way of serious efforts on tasks which are important but are not viewed as immediately topical. Academics who can not make discoveries should still have a task in enlightened teaching—in giving their students educated company.

Perhaps nowhere is the failure of commercial principles in the domain of culture more evident than on television. The "wasteland" is a striking example of social waste: the total resource cost is quite high. Ratings are relative to each other, and if the level is low, ratings are powerless to elicit any improvement. Public television does not seem to be the whole answer either; its dependence on donated funds is a weakness and it seems unable to compete with commercial television for high pay.

One way out might be to divorce advertising on television from the other programs. The newspapers have their advertising pages which many people read independently of other parts of the paper. Why could not commercial television offer advertisers certain advertising hours (or, half hours) when only commercials are shown, for the better education of the public about competing products. Then the networks and stations could use their advertising income on programs of entertainment and education without having to answer to individual sponsoring firms for each program.

To sum up: commercial principles do not work particularly well in the domain of culture. Tenure pay and public subsidies are often necessary. After all, the school system (or the bulk of it) lives on public funds, and the tax exemptions of many private schools are also indirect public subsidies. In the past, the arts were often supported by mecenates, public or privately wealthy. Indirectly, the starving genius whose life's work we all enjoy (courtesy business management, if forthcoming) did in a way subsidize all of us by their lives' sacrifices (who pays Mozart? or Woody Guthrie?) So why should we not, all of us, subsidize some of the benefits they brought the community?

FOOD AND ALL THAT: A PLEA FOR MARKET NEUTRALITY

The food complex, as we emphasized earlier (Chapter 2), is a sizeable case of social waste by its lingering on products which are or will soon be obsolete. It is not by far the greatest case of social waste; if it were the only one, we might even live with it, for on the whole it represents a rear-guard fight rather than a permanent distortion or rigid fixations on unnecessarily high cost levels.

But even so, the total problem of social waste is large, and all savings we can get we should try to get. On food, and other products where obsolescence is shielded from full competition, we would merely ask for equal time: whenever an actor gives a paid performance in favor of natural milk and its derived products, for instance, someone equally gifted at persuading the public should present the case of the alternative products derived from soybeans. At the very least, public agencies such as the Department of Agriculture should abstain from taking sides by telling the public what it wants. In a competitive society, let members of the public themselves say what they want, and let them have objective balanced information on which to make up their minds.

IN DEFENSE OF DEFENSE

Social waste in America has become dangerous because of the energy problem, but this is compounded by the defense issue.

170   *Riches to Rags*

Higher energy and capital costs make a large defense budget heavier to carry. It becomes still heavier by the realization that defense to be realistic must go back to using mainly conventional, non-nuclear weapons. Nuclear weapons in large quantities are too dangerous to use. They deter only nuclear weapons, no longer the use of conventional ones. A country such as the United States must of course continue to have some nuclear deterrent as long as there are any nuclear weapons anywhere in the world. But somehow the nuclear weapons must be reduced to the quantity levels of the 1950's when these weapons were a credible deterrent because they might have been used without burning up the planet. Such a reduced-size deterrent will still be necessary to deter anyone else who otherwise might use this kind of weapons—and we do not necessarily think of another superpower; the danger might as easily come from some "small gangster" among tinhorn dictators, or from terrorists without a country.

But conventional weapons will cost more, so the burden is going to be heavy, now and for some time to come. Cost controls on Department of Defense expenditures will of course have to be tightened considerably, but that will not solve the whole problem which is about real costs as much as about financial ones. (The difference: when a DoD supplier sells the Department a sledgehammer worth $20 for $450, the DoD incurs a financial loss of $430, which is a transfer of money; the real cost is still one sledgehammer). The economy has to give up large amounts of hardware, special materials, energy, highly skilled manpower, and capital. All this is withheld from other production no matter how tightly financial costs are controlled. This is why the defense of defense will call for cutting out large amounts of social waste in the civilian as well as in the military economy. Defending the country requires that the country remains in good shape which it can not be if it is to sustain both civilian social waste and a heavy defense burden at the same time.

BY THE SKIN OF OUR TEETH—
OR THE POWER OF OUR MINDS?

The American economic system needs innovation if it is to survive into an indefinite future, or even to the end of the days of today's youth. In the medium-term past we have been lucky. Now we must forge our own luck by an ingenuity which transcends inherited molds of mind as well as of artifact. Innovations of systems more than of things can not be expected to spring forth without conscious effort from the structures which luck helped put in place. Saying that human ingenuity will take care of all the problems of resource scarcity, by way of the market place, is both disingenious and unhistorical. Historically, there have been many resource crises and catastrophies. Only the modern period has had the appearance of being self-regulating because many essential resources were easily available. As the "petroleum age" now draws toward a close, more will be needed than relying on self-regulating mechanisms. Basically, the economy may very well extricate itself from all its current difficulties and become self-renewing virtually forever. But none of this will happen by itself. It will not happen by merely relying on short-run consumer tastes, or planner tastes, conditioned by the economy as it exists now. Somehow industry must be given a different set of cues to make it obey the longer-run necessities of society as a whole. There will have to be an end to purposeful wastemaking and planned obsolescence. The consequences for society are many. All the systems for employment, income distribution and education for citizenship will have to be thought through afresh and revamped to fit the new realities.

To those who say that a deliberate, concerted and reasonably rapid switch in the general direction discussed here is difficult, there are two answers. One is yes—it is very difficult indeed. The other is that thorough innovation of our economy is the only route toward the future which is not impossible or absurd. The earth may have its limits, but the domain of the human mind is virtually boundless—if only it is free from self-imposed bondage to the habits of thought of past ages.